Communication Strategies 1

by David Paul

CENGAGE
Learning™

Australia • Brazil • Japan • Korea • Mexico • Singapore • Spain • United Kingdom • United States

**Communication Strategies 1
Student Text**

David Paul

Publishing Director:
Paul Tan

Director of Global Marketing:
Ian Martin

Senior Product Manager:
Michael Cahill

Interior Design:
Lynn Dennett

Illustrator:
Ross Thomson

ISBN-13: 978-981-4232-59-3
ISBN-10: 981-4232-59-9

Cengage Learning Asia Pte Ltd
5 Shenton Way #01-01
UIC Building
Singapore 068808

Cengage Learning is a leading provider of customized learning solutions with office locations around the globe, including Singapore, the United Kingdom, Australia, Mexico, Brazil and Japan.

Locate your local office at: **international.cengage.com/region**

Cengage Learning products are represented in Canada by Nelson Education, Ltd.

For product information, visit **cengageasia.com**

The publisher would like to thank The Kobal Collection for their permission to reproduce photographs:

8: Bowfinger — Universal, ph: Zade Rosenthal; 14: The Endless Summer II - New Line Cinema; 20: Little Rascals — Amblin, ph: Melissa Moseley; 26: When a Man Loves a Woman — Touchstone, ph: Peter Sorel; 32: Modern Times - Chaplin/United Artists; 38: Babe: Pig in the City — Universal; 44: Fairytale: A True Story - Icon Productions; 50: Star Trek III The Search for Spock — Paramount; 56: Big Business — MGM; 62: Trainspotting - Figment/Noel gay/Channel 4, ph: Liam Longman; 68: Malcolm X - Warner Brothers, ph: David Lee; 74: K-9 — Universal, ph: Marsha Blackburn; 80: Patriot Games — Paramount, ph: Merrick Morton; 86: Bus Stop - 20th Century Fox; 92: Elizabeth Taylor - MGM

Printed in Singapore
2 3 4 5 6   11 10 09 08

Acknowledgments

I would like to thank:

Everyone at Thomson for their encouragement and belief in the project, especially Guy de Villiers, the development editor, and John Lowe, for recognizing the potential of the course.

Lynn Dennett for the wonderful design and so much hard work.

Brian Elliot for the photographs, and the David English House staff who bravely volunteered to be models.

All those who encouraged this project in the early stages, especially Yvonne de Henseler, Vaughan Jones, Richard Kemp and Mike Esplen.

All the staff and teachers who have been part of David English House in Hiroshima, Seoul and Bangkok over the years. Thank you so much for your support and hard work.

In addition, we would like to extend our thanks to the professionals who have offered invaluable comments and suggestions during the development of the course. Many thanks to those listed below:

David Paul

Carol Rinnert	Hiroshima City University, Hiroshima, Japan
Susan Lee	Lykeion Language Forum, Seoul, South Korea
Alice Svendson	Jumonji Women's College, Tokyo, Japan
Sangdo Woo	Gongju National University of Education, Gongju, South Korea
Michael Guest	Miyazaki Medical College, Miyazaki, Japan
Grace Chang	Tak-Ming Technical College, Taipei, Taiwan
Rob Waring	Notre Dame Seishin University, Okayama, Japan
Michael Wiener	SIAM Computer & Language Institute, Bangkok, Thailand
Kerry Muir	Tokai University Junior College, Tokyo, Japan
Bill Pellowe	Kinki University, Fukuoka, Japan
Sophia Shang	Whatcom College, Bellingham, USA
Jason Kim	BCM Language Institute, Seoul, South Korea
Renee Sawazaki	Rikkyo University, Tokyo, Japan
Stephen Shrader	LIOJ, Odawara, Japan
Professor Kyung-Whan Cha	Chung-Ang University, Seoul, South Korea
Kevin Sawatzky	Nova Futamatagawa School, Kanagawa, Japan
Anne-Marie Hadzima	National Taiwan University, Taipei, Taiwan
Simon Howell	Kansai Gaidai, Osaka, Japan
Linh Thuy Pallos	Kyoto Tachibana Women's University, Kyoto, Japan
David Campbell	JOY Academy, Hokkaido, Japan
Professor Oryang Kwon	Seoul National University, Seoul, South Korea
Michael Bradley	Bradley's English School, Koriyama City, Japan
Thomas Asada Grant	Daito Bunka University, Saitama, Japan
Chia Jung Tang	National Chengchi University, Taipei, Taiwan
Bob Jones	REJ English House, Gifu, Japan
Joseph Wang	Southern Taiwan University of Technology, Tai Nan, Taiwan
David McMurray	The International University of Kagoshima, Kagoshima, Japan
Mark Zeid	Hiroshima Gaigo Senmon Gakko, Hiroshima, Japan
Jean-Louis van der Merwe	KoJen ELS, Taipei, Taiwan
Michael Stout	Universal Language Institute, Tokyo, Japan
Peter Warner	At Home English, Nagoya, Japan
Sarah Tsai-Feng Yin	Caves Educational Training Co Ltd, Taipei, Taiwan
Cory Mcgowan	Yamasa English School, Okazaki, Japan
Gregory Mihaich	New Tokyo School, Kagoshima, Japan
Teachers from:	Shane English Schools, Japan; Lang Education Center, Hiroshima, Japan; Four Seasons Language School and Cultural Center, Hamamatsu, Japan

Table of Contents

	Theme	Points of View	Sample Patterns
1	Friends	I like people that talk a lot	I like people who/that ... I prefer ... I'm fed up with ...
2	Free Time	I love being lazy	I can't understand people who/that ... I don't have time to ... If I were in good shape ...
3	The Past	I played soccer all the time	When I was a child, I ... I could ... when I was ... I used to ...
4	The Family	We should live with elderly relatives	I'd hate it if ... It's our duty to ... Many people don't appreciate ...
5	Work	In my ideal job, I'd have a lot of responsibility	In my ideal job, I'd ... I'm prepared to work overtime if ... I'm fine as long as ...
6	City Life	Cities are noisy and polluted	It sometimes takes hours to ... It gives me a chance to escape from ... I need more chances to ...
7	Beliefs	We can judge a person's character by their blood type	Some people consider me to be ... I don't know why so many people ... I was once taken in by ...
8	The Future	Nobody will have to work	I predict that ... 100 years from now ... In the future, we'll be able to ...
9	Transportation	Driving is a good way to relax	... is a good way to get rid of stress ... makes me irritated People become too dependent on ...
10	Vices	Smoking should be made illegal	I should be allowed to ... The only reason ... Governments should discourage ...
11	Marriage	Weddings shouldn't be extravagant	Some people spend ridiculous ... It's natural for parents to ... It's important for ...
12	Animals	There's no difference between eating cows and whales	I get upset if ... ... are in danger of becoming extinct Most people would be horrified if ...
13	Computers	Computer games are bad for children	I'm in a world of my own ... helps me concentrate ... is bad for our eyesight
14	The Generation Gap	Young people should get steady jobs	... isn't afraid to be different ... follows the crowd ... doesn't get me anywhere
15	Travel	I usually join a tour group	It's often said that ... I want to get to know ... I don't have enough confidence to ...

Strategies	Situation	Collocation Sets
I'm the opposite We are very similar Maybe we aren't so different	Telephoning a friend	Friend Friendship Relationship
I know how you feel, but ... I know what you mean, but ... It may not seem like it, but ...	At a restaurant	Time Trip Restaurant
It sounds like/as if ... It seems like/as if ... It looks like/as if ...	Story telling	Memory Attention Story
It's true that ..., but ... It may be true that ..., but ... That's a good point, but ...	Looking for a house	Family Child Home
You might think differently if ... If I do/did that, I ... I don't care if/whether ... or not	Job interview	Job Work Company
Don't you think ...? Is that why ...? Are you sure ...?	Apologizing with reasons	City Area Countryside
I don't know why ... I have no idea how ... I'm not sure what ...	Trying to convince somebody that you've seen a ghost	Lucky Luck Believe
That/It would lead to ... That/It would mean ... That/It would cause ...	Proposing marriage	Future Dream Hope
You don't know what you're ... That's nonsense! That's ridiculous!	Stopped by the police	Car Traffic Train
It doesn't make sense to ... It's hard to understand/see why ... I don't understand/see why ...	At the doctor	Habit Temptation Gamble
My impression is that ... ... is not as ... as it seems My guess is that ...	Honeymoons	Love Husband Wife
I accept that ..., but ... I admit that ..., but ... I realize that ..., but ...	At the pet shop	Animal Fish Cat
It should be ... It must be ... It can't be ...	At a computer store	Computer Technology E-mail
There's no reason to ... There's no need to ... There's no point in ...	Comparing the past with the present	Generation Age Fashion
I bet ... I doubt if ... I guess ...	Giving a guided tour	Vacation Flight Tourist

Tomoko
Japan

Jin-Sook
Korea

Lee
China

Sonchai
Thailand

Carlos
Brazil

Karima
Kenya

Michelle
Switzerland

Manosh
India

Christina
Sweden

Hassan
Saudi Arabia

1. Friends

WARM-UP QUESTIONS

Think of a good friend.

What do you do together?
What do you talk about?
Why do you like him/her?
In general, what kind of people do you like?

VOCABULARY

Here are some words that will be useful in this unit.
How many do you know?

serious	sincere	humor
selfish	witty	confident
sensitive	easygoing	arrogant
generous	sociable	reliable

Discuss which of the above words could fit in the following gaps.

Tomoko: Carlos has no sense of _____. He's always so _____. I wish he would tell
          a few jokes sometimes.

Jin-Sook: He's just not very _____, and not very _____ either. I think he just prefers being by himself. I really
            like him, though. I just wish he was a bit more _____ in social situations, and he's too _____ so
            he gets hurt easily.

Tomoko: I must admit, he's a great guy! He's a very _____ friend, so I can always depend on him in a crisis.
          Even when I'm extremely _____ and _____, he doesn't seem to mind at all.

What words that are not in the list can you think of to describe your friends?

MIND MAP

Here is Jin-Sook's mind map starting from 'people I like'.

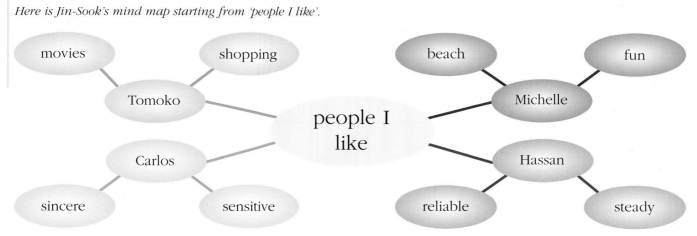

Now make your own mind map with 'people I like' in the center.
Talk about your mind map with another student or the rest of the class.

Bowfinger—Universal, ph: Zade Rosenthal

POINTS OF VIEW - I LIKE PEOPLE THAT TALK A LOT

I like people that are sociable and talk a lot. It's important for them to have a sense of humor, too. I love having lively, witty conversations with friends. I easily get bored when I'm with people who are quiet or shy.

I'm the opposite. I feel much more comfortable when I'm with people who are quiet. I think people that are sociable and witty are often arrogant. I prefer to have friends who stand back and notice what's going on around them. I couldn't have a close friendship or go out with anybody who wasn't sensitive and kind.

It's cool to be a bit arrogant, and I want to hang out with friends that are cool. I might change my mind if I have a serious relationship or want to get married. But right now, I want to have fun.

Maybe we aren't so different. When you get fed up with just having fun, you'll probably start looking for a lot of sensitive friends and a very kind husband. Deep down, you probably want the same things as me.

Practice and Discussion

PERSONALIZATION

Complete these sentences with your own ideas.

I like people that ...
I easily get bored when ...
I feel comfortable when ...
I prefer to have friends that ...
I could never go out with a man/woman that ...
It's cool to ...
I'll probably start looking for ...
I'm fed up with ...

> *I like people that remember my birthday but forget my age.*

"Did you miss me when I was away?"
"Were you away?"

DISCUSSION

> *We are very similar. We both love ice cream!*

DISCUSSION STRATEGIES

I'm the opposite.
We are very similar.
Maybe we aren't so different.

Try to include the discussion strategies and the patterns from the controlled practice section in the following discussions.

Think of somebody you know or a famous person you feel is arrogant.
 Talk about him or her.
Think of somebody you know or a famous person you feel is too sensitive.
 Talk about him or her.
Do you prefer quiet people or people who talk a lot? Why?
When do you feel bored?
What kind of man/woman would you like to have a deep relationship with?
Deep down, what do you really want in your life?

Activities

Make three sentences about your character.

Examples: I'm often selfish.
                I have a great sense of humor!
                I'm a bit arrogant.

Now talk to another student and ask at least two follow-up questions about each point.

Examples:
A: When are you selfish?
B: When I'm tired in the evening.
A: What do you do that's so selfish?
B: I just play computer games and hardly talk to anybody.

Student A: TV reporter. Interview Student B about his/her friends.
Student B: Play the role of a famous person.

Example questions:
Who are your best friends?
When did you first meet?
What do you usually do together?
What do you think of (name of another famous person)?

SITUATION - TELEPHONING A FRIEND

Brainstorming: *Think of expressions we often use on the telephone.*
                   Think of ways to ask somebody for a date.
                   Think of ways to refuse an invitation.

Student A: *Telephone B and ask him/her out to seven different places over the next week.*

Examples:
Are you doing anything on Monday night?
I'm thinking of eating out on Tuesday night.
Would you like to come, too?

Student B: *Refuse the first six invitations, giving a different reason each time. Accept the last invitation.*

Examples:
I'm sorry, I'm busy on Monday. I'll be getting ready for a test.
I wish I could, but I have to go to the gym.
I'd love to come. Thank you for asking.

"*Why don't we go window shopping?*"
"*I don't want to buy any windows.*"

1. Friends

Further Activities

Put the following into sentences or dialogues:

Friend
1. make friends   *Example:*   I've made a lot of new friends since I started learning English.
2. best friend
3. a friend of the family

Friendship
1. develop a friendship   *Example:*   If we have more opportunities to develop our friendship, we might end up getting married.
2. a close friendship
3. a token of friendship

Relationship
1. a love-hate relationship
> A: We have a love-hate relationship.
> B: You mean you love her, but she hates you?
> A: No, I mean it's very passionate. Sometimes we get along great, and at other times we fight all the time.

2. a deep relationship
3. a serious relationship

Prepare a short speech on one of these three topics:

A misunderstanding with a friend.
We should love our enemies.
My ideal boyfriend, girlfriend, husband or wife.

Put the following into short dialogues:

bump into   on the tip of my tongue
long time no see   between you and me

Example:
> A: I bumped into Maria last week. She said she's found a new job.
> B: That's good news. I know she hated her previous job.

"Waiter! What's the matter with this fish?"
"Long time no sea, sir."

Consolidation & Recycling

Across

3 I want to ___ looking for a new job.
6 I'm ___ selfish when I'm at home.
7 Are you doing anything ___ Monday night?
9 She's very ___. Anything is OK.
11 I must ___, he's a great guy.
13 I like people who ___ what's going on around them.
17 He doesn't seem to ___ at all.
19 He's very sensitive. He gets hurt ___.
20 What kind of people ___ you like?
22 I don't want to buy ___ windows.
23 I can always ___ on him in a crisis.

Down

1 He's ___ serious. He needs to relax.
2 I'll be getting ___ for a test.
3 He's so ___. He only thinks about himself.
4 She's so ___! She thinks she's so beautiful!
5 I couldn't go out with anybody who wasn't ___ and kind.
8 Long ___ no see.
10 I couldn't ___ out with anybody that wasn't kind.
12 I prefer to have friends who ___ back and notice what's going on.
14 ___ when I'm selfish, he doesn't seem to mind.
15 ___ somebody for a date.
16 I couldn't have a ___ friendship with him.
17 It's a good way to ___ friends.
18 Deep ___, you probably want the same things as me.
21 I'm ___ up with just having fun.

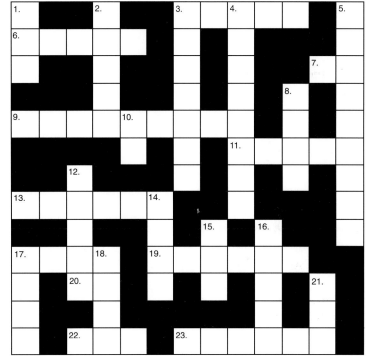

Write eight separate sentences, each of which includes both words in the pairs below:

like / people   notice / what
sense / humor   deep / relationship
feel / comfortable   sensitive / quiet
make / friends   prefer / have

Write paragraphs about the following. Try to include words and patterns from this unit.

People I like.
Being a good friend.
Good ways to make new friends.

Which section of the unit did you find most interesting?
In which section of the unit did you learn the most?
Make a list of any new words and patterns from this unit that you want to try and remember.
You may find it helpful to write each word or pattern on a card.

2. Free Time

WARM-UP QUESTIONS

How much free time do you have?
What do you usually do in your free time?
What do you dislike doing in your free time?
If you had a lot of money, what would you do in your free time?

VOCABULARY

Here are some words and expressions that will be useful in this unit.
How many do you know?

eat out	out of shape	lazy
in good shape	take a trip	exhausted
opportunity	calm down	waste
fond of	rush around	take care of

Discuss which of the above words and expressions could fit in the following gaps.

Lee: I don't have much free time, and I tend to ____ doing a lot of things. I don't like to ____ time.

Christina: I'm very different. I work very hard, too, so when I have free time I feel ____ and just want to stay home. I like to ___ my pets and plants. They really help me ___ and feel relaxed.

Lee: I'm ___ pets, too, but I prefer using my free time actively to staying at home. I often ____ at nice restaurants, and use every _____ I have to ____ somewhere.

What words/phrases that are not in the list can you think of that might be useful when we talk about free time?

MIND MAP

Here is Christina's mind map starting from 'free time'.

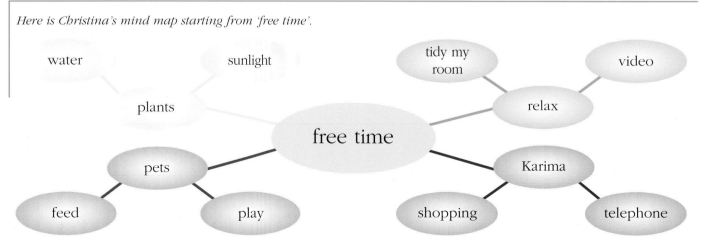

Now make your own mind map with 'free time', 'fun', 'sports', or 'hobbies' in the center.
Talk about your mind map with another student or the rest of the class.

The Endless Summer II—New Line Cinema

POINTS OF VIEW - I LOVE BEING LAZY!

I love being lazy! It's wonderful to lie on the beach all day or relax in front of the TV watching one of my favorite videos. I also like taking walks, and occasionally play tennis or golf, but I can't understand people that go to the gym all the time.

I understand how you feel, but you don't know what it's like to be in good shape! It's such a fantastic feeling! I go to the gym every evening after work. First I do some weight training, then I do some aerobics or go for a swim in the pool. I look forward to it all day.

But it's such hard work! How can you enjoy so much pain? And there are so many other things to do in the evening. You can't have time to eat out or go to the movies. I can't imagine liking weight training more than a delicious Italian pizza! I go out for dinner or go to a movie with my friends almost every night. You must be too exhausted to do that kind of thing.

It may not seem like it, but I find I have a lot of energy to do other things as well. I often eat out, too. I don't go to movies very often, but I do like going dancing or bowling. If I was out of shape, I wouldn't have the energy to do so much.

2. Free Time

Practice and Discussion

PERSONALIZATION

Complete these sentences with your own ideas.

I think it's wonderful to ...
I can't understand people that ...
... is such a fantastic feeling!
I look forward to ... all day.
... is such hard work!
I don't have time to ...
I can't imagine ...
If I were/weren't in good shape ...

I can't understand people that are unkind to animals.

"I can play the violin by ear."
"Don't your earrings get in the way?"

DISCUSSION

It may not seem like it, but I don't enjoy shopping.

DISCUSSION STRATEGIES

I understand/know how you feel, but ...
I understand/see/know what you mean, but ...
It may not seem like it, but ...

Try to include the discussion strategies and the patterns from the controlled practice section in the following discussions.

Where do you like to eat out?
Do you have a good balance between work/studying and free time? Talk about it.
Do you try to keep in good shape? If so, how? If not, why not?
Who do you know that rushes around a lot?
   Talk about how he/she could relax more.
What would you like to do but don't have time to do?
Do you mind wasting time?
Do you think it is necessary to do things that are hard or painful?

Activities

FOLLOW-UP QUESTIONS

List three things you often do in your free time.

Examples: I telephone my friends.
                 I go to see movies.
                 I go shopping.

*Now talk to another student and ask at least
two follow-up questions about each point.*

Examples:

A: How often do you telephone your friends?
B: Every evening.
A: What kinds of things do you talk about?
B: We talk about what our friends are doing,
           our plans for the weekend. We just like chatting.

ROLE PLAY

Student A: *TV reporter. Interview Student B
about the exercise he/she takes.*
Student B: *Be yourself or play the role of a
famous person.*

Example questions:
What kind of exercise do you take?
Is it enough?
Are there any new sports you'd like to take up?

SITUATION - AT A RESTAURANT

Brainstorming: *Think of your ideal menu.
Think of ways to ask for things on the menu.
Think of ways a waiter may say no to your requests.*

Student A: *You are a customer in a restaurant. Order dinner.
Complain when the food you order is not available, and after you receive your food.*

Examples:
What do you mean 'it's not available'? It's on the menu.
I asked for chicken, but this is duck.
Well, what do you recommend?

Student B: *You are a waiter. Most of the food
A orders is not available today.*

Examples:
I'm extremely sorry, sir/madam,
   I'll get you a clean one.
I'm very sorry. We've just run out of champagne.
I'm afraid that's a typing mistake.
   It should say 'duck'.

"Why is my hamburger flat?"
"Well, sir, you said 'I want a hamburger, and step on it!'"

2. Free Time

Further Activities

COLLOCATION SETS

Put the following into sentences or dialogues:

Time
1. save time
2. run out of time
3. kill time

Example: We'll save time if we take a short cut.

Trip
1. arrange a trip
2. cancel a trip
3. a business trip

Example: We've arranged a trip to Hawaii. Everybody's going!

Restaurant
1. a crowded restaurant

Example: You have to reserve a table in advance.
The restaurant gets crowded very early.

2. a local restaurant
3. a traditional restaurant

SPEECHES

Prepare a short speech on one of these three topics:

It's important to have a lot of free time.
Watching TV is bad for us.
Sports should be amateur, not professional.

EXTRA EXPRESSIONS

Put the following into short dialogues:

take it easy   running / in a row
practice makes perfect   so far so good

Example:
A: How's your training course going?
B: Well, so far so good, but it's getting more difficult
       all the time.

"Does your husband take a lot of exercise?"
"Yes, last week he went out five nights
running."

Consolidation & Recycling

BUILDING VOCABULARY

Across

1 I have a lot of ___ to do other things as well.
3 It may not ___ like it.
7 She's very ___. She knows she will do well.
9 I love having ___ conversations with friends.
11 He's so ___. He never tells jokes.
12 I ___ I could, but I have to go to the gym.
14 I went on a business ___ to Bangkok.
18 Who would you like to have a ___ relationship with?
19 Would you like to ___, too?
20 It's great to ___ on the beach.
21 I often ___ ___ at nice restaurants.
22 I love being ___!

Down

1 After working hard, I feel ___.
2 He's so ___. He's always giving things to people.
4 What are you doing this ___?
5 When I was a child, I ___ studied hard.
6 It's on the ___ of my tongue.
8 You'll have to reserve a place. It gets ___ early.
10 I'm ___ sorry, sir.
13 We had to ___ the trip to Paris.
15 I ___ being by myself.
16 Waiter! May I have the ___, please?
17 I like to ___ my free time actively.

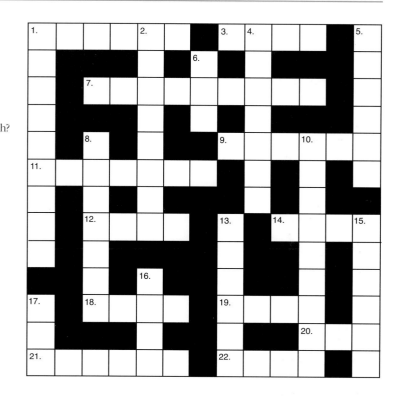

FOCUSING ON COLLOCATIONS

Write eight separate sentences, each of which includes both words in the pairs below:

wonderful / to   good / shape
fed / up   go / out
have / time   selfish / arrogant
cool / to   local / restaurant

WRITING OPINIONS

Write paragraphs about the following. Try to include words and patterns from this unit.

The importance of doing exercise.
How to relax.
Balancing work/studying and free time.

REFLECTION

Which section of the unit did you find most interesting?
In which section of the unit did you learn the most?
Make a list of any new words and patterns from this unit that you want to try and remember.
You may find it helpful to write each word or pattern on a card.

3. The Past

WARM-UP QUESTIONS

What did you like doing when you were younger?
What did you want to be when you were younger?
How is your life now better than it was in the past?
How is your life now worse than it was in the past?

VOCABULARY

Here are some words and expressions that will be useful in this unit.
How many do you know?

used to	had to	out of date
grew up	miss	memory
traditional	old-fashioned	regret
didn't let	remind me of	brought up

Discuss which of the above words and expressions could fit in the following gaps.

Manosh: I guess I'm _____. I was _____ in a very ____ family, and I don't easily adapt to new ways of doing things.

Tomoko: It sounds like you don't have much fun! When I was a child I always ____ study, and my parents _____ me play in the evenings, so now I just like having fun and keeping up with the latest fashions. As soon as something's ____, I'm not interested in it any more.

Manosh: You _____ my sister. She's just like you! I think you'll _____ it later, and wish you had been more interested in culture and history and not just in temporary fashions.

What words/phrases that are not in the list can you think of that might be useful when we talk about the past?

MIND MAP

Here is Tomoko's mind map starting from 'when I was a child'.

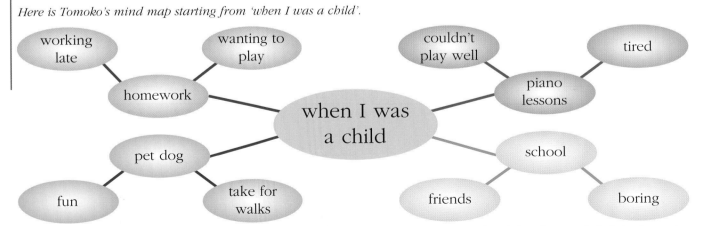

Now make your own mind map with 'when I was a child', '5 years ago', '10 years ago' or 'when I was a baby' in the center.
Talk about your mind map with another student or the rest of the class.

Little Rascals—Amblin, ph: Melissa Moseley

POINTS OF VIEW - I PLAYED SOCCER ALL THE TIME

When I was a child, I played soccer all the time. And I used to go and watch our local soccer team whenever they had a home game.

You remind me of my brother. The only thing he ever thought about was soccer. It was so boring. And he was so good at it! He was always the center of attention! I used to prefer going to the beach. I could swim when I was four, and I could surf well when I was about ten. I always had a tan and I was always active.

It sounds like you'll get skin cancer! It's dangerous for children to spend so much time outside. I spent most of my time indoors. Whenever I could, I'd go to a room above our garage. Nobody else used that room, so I painted pictures and took care of my pets. It was great! I have so many happy memories of playing in that room.

It sounds as if you didn't get much fresh air! And it seems like none of you spent much time with adults. I spent most of my time with older people. I think it made me interested in things children of my age normally don't pay much attention to. I used to read a lot as well, so maybe that's why I'm quite a serious person. I wonder if children who spend most of their time with other children or by themselves ever really grow up.

3. The Past

Practice and Discussion

PERSONALIZATION

Complete these sentences with your own ideas.

When I was a child, I spent as much time as possible ...
I could ... when I was ...
I used to prefer ... to ...
It's dangerous for children to ...
Whenever I can/could, I ...
Nobody else ...
I don't pay much attention to ...
I used to ... Maybe that's why I'm ...

I could play soccer well when I was five.

"When I was a child I had a pet dachshund called Johannes Sebastian."
"That's an unusual name. Why did you call him that?"
"He was very noisy. It was short for Johannes Sebastian Bark."

DISCUSSION

It looks like you're working hard.

DISCUSSION STRATEGIES

It sounds like/as if ...
It seems like/as if ...
It looks like/as if ...

Try to include the discussion strategies and the patterns from the controlled practice section in the following discussions.

What were you like as a child?
Were you happier as a child than you are now? Why?
What did you used to like doing that you don't do any more?
Who most influenced you as a child? In which ways?
In which ways are you traditional?
What do you miss from your past?
What things do you regret about the past?

Activities

FOLLOW-UP QUESTIONS

List three of the favorite toys you had when you were a child.

Examples: I had a favorite teddy bear.
I had a train set.
I had a computer race game
    I played all the time.

Now talk to another student and ask at least two follow-up questions about each point.

Examples:
A: What was your teddy bear like?
B: It was small, and brown and very soft.
A: Did you sleep with it?
B: Sometimes, but I usually kicked him out of bed in the middle of the night.

ROLE PLAY

Student A: *TV reporter. Interview Student B about his/her primary school.*
Student B: *Be yourself or play the role of a famous person.*

Example questions:
Who was your favorite teacher?
Did you join any clubs?
Did you go on any excursions?

SITUATION - STORY TELLING

Brainstorming: *See if there are any famous fairy stories most of the class know well.*
See if there are any famous movies or TV serials almost all the class know.
See if there are any books almost all the class have read.

The class is in two teams. Tell a story sentence by sentence. Each of you says a sentence in turn, alternating between teams. If you cannot make a sentence within a time limit, the other team gets a point.

Examples:
Once upon a time ...
Some time later ...
A little while after that ...
But before that happened ...
The next day ...
And they all lived happily ever after.

"Once upon a time there was a beautiful princess ..."
"... with a wooden leg ..."
"... called Diana ..."
"... and her other leg was called Tom ..."

3. The Past

Further Activities

COLLOCATION SETS

Put the following into sentences or dialogues:

Memory

1. a terrible memory   *Example:*   I have a terrible memory, especially for people's names.
2. a happy memory
3. a vague memory

Attention

1. pay attention   *Example:*   I usually don't pay much attention when my mother lectures me.
2. the center of attention
3. attract attention

Story

1. tell a story   *Example:*   I'll tell you a story about something that happened to me when I was a child.

2. a true story
3. a fairy story

SPEECHES

Prepare a short speech on one of these three topics:

Childhood is the happiest time of our lives.
Music isn't as good as it used to be.
We should always move forward. We should never look back.

EXTRA EXPRESSIONS

Put the following into short dialogues:

in the long run   for the time being
cut down   better late than never

Example:

A: Do you like where you're living?
B: It's all right for the time being, but sooner or later I'm going to move to a nicer place.

"You haven't changed in five years!"
"I'm trying to cut down on laundry bills."

Consolidation & Recycling

BUILDING VOCABULARY

Across

1   A ___ friend always supports you.
4   She has a wonderful ___ of humor.
6   Young people think my ideas are out of ___.
7   I go to the gym ___ work.
8   We fight all the ___.
10 I have a ___ rabbit.
12 I like to do weight ___ at the gym.
13 I played on a baseball ___.
15 She ___ every opportunity she has.
17 When I was a child, I ___ ___ read a lot.
19 My parents didn't ___ me stay up late.
21 She likes being by ___.
22 Everything will be fine in the ___ run.
23 I ___ if she is happy.

Down

1   My family are very ___. They aren't modern at all.
2   The only thing she ___ thought about was volleyball.
3   I bumped into Maria ___ week.
4   It ___ like none of you do much exercise.
5   You are all out of ___.
9   I have a ___ memory of meeting him a long time ago.
11 ___ fashions soon change.
14 We might ___ up getting married.
16 If we go this way, we'll ___ a lot of time.
18 I ___ too much time at my computer.
20 I went to the beach a lot, and always had a ___.

FOCUSING ON COLLOCATIONS

Write eight separate sentences, each of which includes both words in the pairs below:

when / child   brought / up
looking / for   take / care
run / out   easily / get
spend / time   pay / attention

WRITING OPINIONS

Write paragraphs about the following. Try to include words and patterns from this unit.

When I was a child.
People and things I miss.
Regrets.

REFLECTION

Which section of the unit did you find most interesting?
In which section of the unit did you learn the most?
Make a list of any new words and patterns from this unit that you want to try and remember.
You may find it helpful to write each word or pattern on a card.

4. The Family

WARM-UP QUESTIONS

How many brothers and sisters would you like to have? Why?
Which members of your family do you feel closest to? Why?
How well do/did you know your grandparents?
What kinds of things do/did you talk about with your parents?

VOCABULARY

Here are some words and expressions that will be useful in this unit.
How many do you know?

cousins	relatives	descended from
look after	unreasonable	depend on
spoil	criticize	appreciate
sacrifice	responsibility	in-law

Discuss which of the above words and expressions could fit in the following gaps.

Michelle: I can't live at home. My parents ____ me almost all the time. It may sound like I don't ___ everything they've done for me, but I just want to be free to be myself. Besides, my older sister and her husband are at home and I can't stand my brother _____.

Karima: I don't live at home either, but for different reasons. My parents used to ___ me so much. They would give me almost anything I wanted, and ____ what they wanted, so that I would be happy. I left home because I didn't want to ____ them any more.

Michelle: My sister and her husband are going to live in Hawaii, and all my _____ and other _____ are scattered all over the place, so I think it's going to be me who will ____ my parents when they get older. I wonder if I'll have the strength to be a good daughter.

What words/phrases that are not in the list can you think of that might be useful when we talk about our families?

MIND MAP

Here is Michelle's mind map starting from 'parents getting old'.

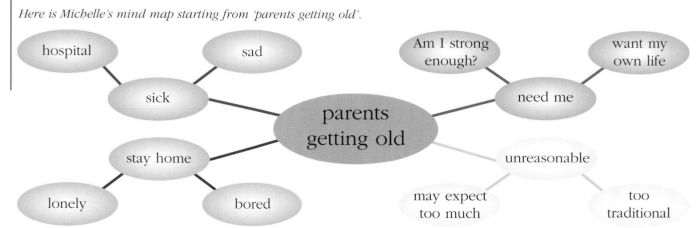

Now make your own mind map with 'parents getting old', 'my family', 'my parents' or 'my future family' in the center.
Talk about your mind map with another student or the rest of the class.

When a Man Loves a Woman—Touchstone, ph: Peter Sorel

POINTS OF VIEW - WE SHOULD LIVE WITH ELDERLY RELATIVES

I live with my two sisters, my parents and two of my grandparents. We're one big happy family! I'd hate it if my grandparents had to live by themselves or in a special home for old people. I think it's our duty to look after our parents when they get older. After all, they made many sacrifices for us when we were children.

You're living in the past! It's true that we owe our parents a lot, but nowadays it's normal for children and their parents to live in different cities or even in different countries. Old people who expect to live with their children's families are being selfish and unreasonable.

It may be true that many families can't help becoming scattered, but we can often find a way to live with our parents after they become old if we try hard enough. It's often the children who are selfish and don't appreciate how much their parents have done for them.

In modern society, the government should be responsible for taking care of old people. Maybe we should all pay more tax, so that homes for old people can be as nice as possible.

4. The Family

Practice and Discussion

PERSONALIZATION

Complete these sentences with your own ideas.

I live with ...
I'd hate it if ...
It's our duty to ...
It's normal to ...
I can't help ...
We can ... if we try hard enough.
Many people don't appreciate ...
I'm responsible for ...

I live with my dog and cat.

"Am I descended from a gorilla?"
"I'm not sure. I don't know your father's family very well."

DISCUSSION

It's true that I spend too much money on fashionable clothes.

DISCUSSION STRATEGIES
It's true that ... but ...
It may be true that ... but ...
That's a good point, but ...

Try to include the discussion strategies and the patterns from the controlled practice section in the following discussions.

How do you feel about being with people older than you?
Talk about the general situation in your family.
Do you think the typical family life in your country has changed a lot in recent years? How? Why?
How do/would you feel about living with your partner's parents after marriage? Why?
How can society pay for the increasing number of old people?
Are the old or the young usually more selfish? Why?
How do you want to live when you get older?

Activities

FOLLOW-UP QUESTIONS

List three things you know about your family's history.

Examples: My grandparents lived in China.
Most of my ancestors were farmers.
My family used to be rich.

*Now talk to another student and ask each at least two
follow-up questions about each point.*

Examples:

A: Which part of China did they live in?
B: I think it was in the north.
A: Why were they living there?
B: They were Chinese, and they left China
to live in Thailand.

ROLE PLAY

Student A: TV reporter. Interview Student B.
Student B: Pretend to be a different member
of your family.

Example questions:
What do you do every day?
What do you think of (Student B)?

SITUATION - LOOKING FOR A HOUSE

Brainstorming: Think of nice places to live in your city.
Think of nice places to live around the world.
Think of qualities a nice house should have.

Student A: You are at a real estate agency looking for a house for your family.

Examples:
I'm looking for a small house that isn't too far from the station.
What's the neighborhood like?
Is there enough space in the living room for
my tank of piranha?

Student B: You are working in the agency.

Examples:
There's a convenience store just around the corner.
It was redecorated and completely rewired last year.
There's a nice view from the bedroom.

"It's only a stone's throw from the bus stop."
"That's good. When we have nothing to do
we can throw stones at the buses."

4. The Family

Further Activities

COLLOCATION SETS

Put the following into sentences or dialogues:

Family

1. support a family   *Example:*   My father and mother both work to support the family.
2. a talented family
3. a single-parent family

Child

1. a spoiled child   *Example:*   I was definitely a spoiled child. I could have almost anything I wanted.
2. a naughty child
3. have a child

Home

1. leave home   *Example:*   I want to leave home and live by myself. / I usually leave home at 7:30.

2. a comfortable home
3. work from home

SPEECHES

Prepare a short speech on one of these three topics:

Families are only important when we are children.
Most parents spoil young children too much.
Parents should give teenagers a lot of freedom.

EXTRA EXPRESSIONS

Put the following into short dialogues:

black sheep of the family   take after
run in the family   make yourself at home

Example:
A: Who do you take after?
B: I'm not really sure. I think I take after my father more than my mother.

"Dancers run in the family."
"It's a pity they don't dance."

Consolidation & Recycling

BUILDING VOCABULARY

Across

1   We are ___. We both like animals a lot.
3   I won't ___ up my children in a traditional way.
6   You're ___ in the past!
8   I can't ___ going to the gym every night!
10 I played many kinds of sports, so I was always ___.
13 I used to read a lot as ___.
15 Old people shouldn't ___ to live with their children.
16 I'm ___ up with just having fun.
17 I could ___ go out with a man that smokes.
19 It's ___ to be arrogant.
22 When I relax, I like to ___ my room.
23 My best friend and I play tennis ___.

Down

1   My parents would ___ what they wanted so I could be happy.
2   I'm afraid that's a typing ___.
4   We've ___ out of time.
5   I ___ I'm old fashioned.
7   My ___ boyfriend would be very kind.
9   How is your ___ now better than it was in the past?
11 I couldn't have a ___ relationship with her.
12 Nobody ___ used that room.
14 I have a terrible ___. I always forget important things.
16 It sounds like you didn't get much __ air.
18 Let's take a short ___.
20 They didn't ___ me play very much.
21 So ___ so good.

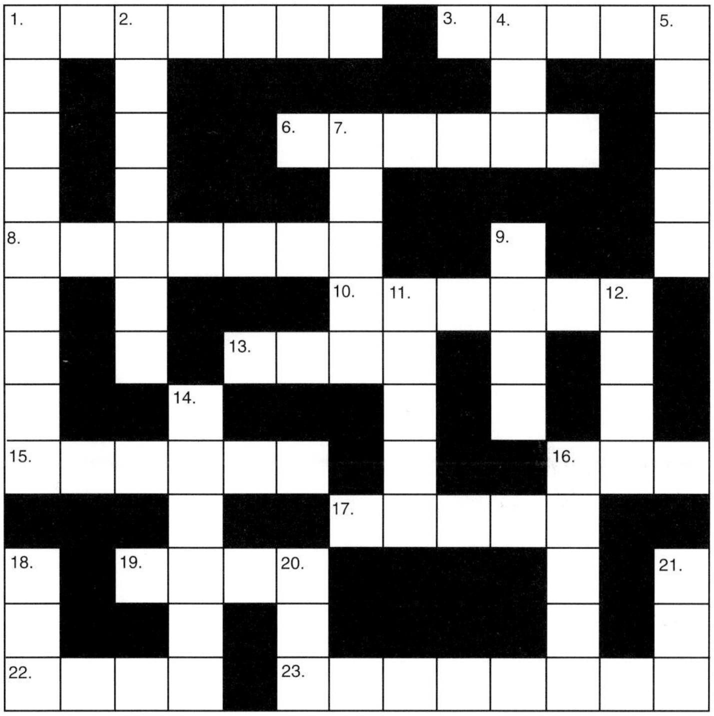

FOCUSING ON COLLOCATIONS

Write eight separate sentences, each of which includes both words in the pairs below:

leave / home   wonder / if
spoilt / child   hate / if
it / important   calm / down
depend / on   not / appreciate

WRITING OPINIONS

Write paragraphs about the following. Try to include words and patterns from this unit.

My parents.
Bringing up children.
Taking care of parents when they are old.

REFLECTION

Which section of the unit did you find most interesting?
In which section of the unit did you learn the most?
Make a list of any new words and patterns from this unit that you want to try and remember.
You may find it helpful to write each word or pattern on a card.

5. Work

WARM-UP QUESTIONS

What part-time or full-time jobs have you done?

When you were a child what did you want to be? Why?

What job wouldn't you want to do? Why?

List five things that make people happy at work (*Example:* long vacations).

VOCABULARY

Here are some words and expressions that will be useful in this unit.
How many do you know?

overtime	civil servant	paperwork
promoted	excitement	self-employed
in charge of	monotonous	manager
laid off	steady	ambition

Discuss which of the above words and expressions could fit in the following gaps.

Hassan: I was _____ last month, so now I'm a _____. I'm _____ the office computer system.

Karima: So you work in an office? I couldn't do that! I'm sure I'd hate working for a large corporation or being a _____. I need more _____ in my life.

Michelle: Having a _____ office job is not so bad. It's not just _____. A lot of my colleagues have become my best friends, and we have a lot of fun together. Though, to be honest, my ___ is to have my own business. I think being _____ will be more secure in the long run. When working for a large corporation, there's always the danger of being _____.

What words/phrases that are not in the list can you think of that might be useful when we talk about work?

MIND MAP

Here is Hassan's mind map starting from 'ideal job'.

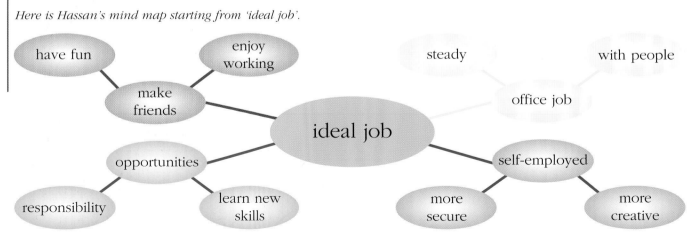

Now make your own mind map with 'ideal job', 'my job', 'my school', or 'part-time jobs' in the center.
Talk about your mind map with another student or the rest of the class.

Modern Times—Chaplin/United Artists

POINTS OF VIEW - IN MY IDEAL JOB, I'D HAVE A LOT OF RESPONSIBILITY

In my ideal job, I'd have many opportunities to travel and meet interesting people. I'd also have a lot of responsibility and be able to take long vacations. I'd be prepared to do a lot of overtime because I'd enjoy what I was doing.

That kind of job wouldn't suit me. I'd be away from home too much. I'd prefer to spend more time with my family. If I traveled a lot and worked long hours, there wouldn't be enough time to build a happy home.

I think it would depend on who your partner was. You might think differently if you married somebody who also worked hard and had a lot of responsibility. You might not see a lot of each other, but that might keep your relationship fresh.

If I had that kind of marriage, we wouldn't have much of a home. I want to have children, and I want them to see a lot of me. I'd be happy with a steady nine to five job. I'd be fine as long as I had a reasonable salary, and could work in an office with a nice atmosphere. I don't care if I have responsibility or not.

Practice and Discussion

PERSONALIZATION

Complete these sentences with your own ideas.

In my ideal job, I'd be able to ...
I'd like to have more opportunities to ...
I'm prepared to work overtime if ...
... doesn't suit me.
I'd like to spend more time ...
If I ..., I wouldn't have enough time to ...
I want/wanted to marry a man/woman who ...
I'm fine as long as ...

Blue doesn't suit me.

"I can't come to work today. I have a very bad sore throat."
"So why aren't you whispering?"
"Is it a secret?"

DISCUSSION

I don't care if I get married or not.

DISCUSSION STRATEGIES

You might think differently if ...
If I do/did that (what you suggest), I ...
I don't care if/whether ... or not.

Try to include the discussion strategies and the patterns from the controlled practice section in the following discussions.

How do you feel about working hard? Why?
Would you like to have a steady office job? Why?
Is it better to be self-employed or work for a large corporation? Why? ✓
What are the advantages and disadvantages of being a civil servant?
Do you want to have responsibility and power? Why? ✓
Do you want your husband/wife to work hard and have responsibility? Why?
Do you think it's important for husbands and wives to see a lot of each other? Why? ✓

Activities

FOLLOW-UP QUESTIONS

List three qualities of a good boss.

Examples: A good boss should try to understand me.
A good boss shouldn't get angry.
A good boss should treat male and
    female employees equally.

*Now talk to another student and ask at least
two follow-up questions about each point.*

Examples:

A: In which ways should your boss
  try to understand you?
B: Well, if I make a mistake, my boss should
  understand that I'm human.
A: What if the mistake is important?
B: Everybody makes mistakes. Even bosses do!

ROLE PLAY

Student A: *TV reporter. Interview Student B
about his/her ambitions.*
Student B: *Be yourself or a famous person.*

Example questions:
What are your ambitions?
Why do you want to be an actress?

SITUATION - JOB INTERVIEW

Brainstorming: *Think of typical questions a job interviewer might ask.*
Think of positive things to say about yourself.
Think of typical questions you could ask a job interviewer.

Student A: *You are interviewing Student B for a job as a salesperson. Your company makes helicopters.*

Examples:
What qualifications do you have?
Have you ever done this kind of work before?
Tell me more about why you like helicopters so much?

Student B: *You are trying to get the job.*

Examples:
I'd like to know more about how much traveling
 I would do.
Who will be the main customers?
I feel confident that I can sell lots of helicopters.

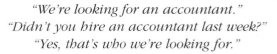

"We're looking for an accountant."
"Didn't you hire an accountant last week?"
"Yes, that's who we're looking for."

5. Work

Further Activities

COLLOCATION SETS

Put the following into sentences or dialogues:

Job
1. apply for a job   *Example:*   I applied for a job at the new department store, but I didn't get it.
2. a badly-paid job
3. a secure job

Work
1. come home from work   *Example:*   I usually come home from work after nine o'clock.
2. concentrate on (my) work
3. take time off work

Company
1. a medium-sized company   *Example:*   I work for a medium-sized company. It has about 40 employees.
2. a dynamic company
3. a subsidiary company

SPEECHES

Prepare a short speech on one of these three topics:

All work and no play makes Jack a dull boy.
It is our duty to work hard.
People should be paid according to ability, not experience.

EXTRA EXPRESSIONS

Put the following into short dialogues:

at/on short notice   get behind
show up late   in advance

Example:
A: I'm sorry to tell you at/on such short notice, but
       I need this translation done by tomorrow night.
B: I'll do my best.

*"You'd better keep away from that bacon slicer.
We're getting a little behind with our orders."*

Consolidation & Recycling

BUILDING VOCABULARY

Across

1. I have always ___ how much my parents did for me.
7. I always ___ what's going on around me.
8. My best friend has a ___ crocodile.
10. Some children spend so much time by ___.
12. ___ upon a time …
14. Who was ___ favorite teacher?
15. Long time ___ see.
16. It's ___ for families to become scatttered.
17. It runs in ___ family.
19. ___, to be honest, I don't know.
22. Make ___ at home.
23. I ___ confident that I can sell a lot.

Down

1. My ___ is to have my own computer business.
2. Waiter! What do you ___?
3. Even when it's noisy, she always ___ on her work.
4. I'm always ___. I never stay at home.
5. ___ down, I think you know I'm right.
6. Red doesn't ___ me.
9. We can find a way if we try hard ___.
11. I get bored when I'm with people that are quiet or ___.
13. ___ else used that room.
17. ___ are so many things to do!
18. We might ___ up getting married.
20. The ___ thing he thought about was work.
21. In the long ___.

FOCUSING ON COLLOCATIONS

Write eight separate sentences, each of which includes both words in the pairs below:

try / hard	serious / relationship
apply / job	care / if
save / time	enough / time
do / overtime	in / charge

WRITING OPINIONS

Write paragraphs about the following. Try to include words and patterns from this unit.

My ideal job.
A good boss.
A job I've done (either full or part time).

REFLECTION

Which section of the unit did you find most interesting?
In which section of the unit did you learn the most?
Make a list of any new words and patterns from this unit that you want to try and remember.
You may find it helpful to write each word or pattern on a card.

6. City Life

WARM-UP QUESTIONS

Why do many people like to live in big cities?
Name one city in each of the five different continents.
Which of these cities would you most like to visit? Why?
Which of these cities would you least like to visit? Why?

VOCABULARY

Here are some words and expressions that will be useful in this unit.
How many do you know?

commute	pollution	amenities
traffic jam	stimulating	glamorous
crowded	materialistic	population
get things done	suburbs	environment

Discuss which of the above words and expressions could fit in the following gaps.

Christina: I live in the _____ of a large city. If I'm lucky it only takes twenty minutes to _____ to work, but when there's a _____ it can take up to two hours! So I go by train, but it's often difficult to get a seat because the train is so _____.

Manosh: I live in a city, too, and the _____ around my house is not very good. Everything's made of concrete! And there are hardly any trees. But the local _____ are good. There are a lot of good shops, and there's a gym nearby.

Christina: The only good thing I can say about the city is that it's good for my work. The surprising thing about living in the city is that even though it has such a large _____, and there are many _____ things to do, I feel much lonelier than I did when I lived in a small town.

What words/phrases that are not in the list can you think of that might be useful when we talk about cities?

MIND MAP

Here is Christina's mind map starting from 'cities'.

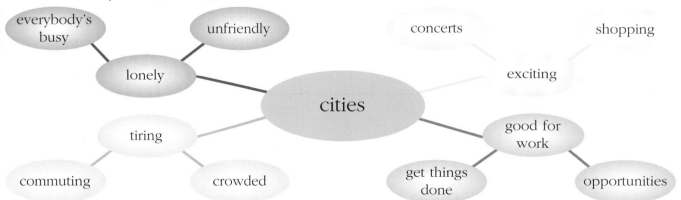

Now make your own mind map with 'cities', 'the countryside', 'my city', or the name of a city (e.g. New York, London, Tokyo…) in the center. Talk about your mind map with another student or the rest of the class.

POINTS OF VIEW - CITIES ARE NOISY AND POLLUTED

Why do so many people want to live in big cities? They're noisy and polluted, people are often unfriendly, and it sometimes takes hours to commute to work. Living in the country or a small town is so much nicer!

For many people there's no choice. There are many more jobs in the cities than in country areas. And for young people, cities offer a chance to escape from a routine life to something more glamorous. There just aren't enough exciting opportunities in the country or small towns.

Is that why they dress in ridiculous fashions and spend all their time discussing pop music or the latest electronic gadgets? It's not glamorous! It's just materialistic and shallow! I just feel sorry for people who go to big cities and get drawn into that kind of world. If they stayed in the country, they'd be much healthier, both physically and mentally.

Don't you think we need a chance to experience city life while we are young, and maybe even be materialistic for a while? Then we can make up our own minds about what's important in life.

6. City Life

Practice and Discussion

PERSONALIZATION

Complete these sentences with your own ideas.

It sometimes takes hours to ...
I ... because there is/was no choice.
... gives me a chance to escape from ...
I think ... is exciting.
I think ... is materialistic.
I feel sorry for ...
I need more chances to ...
I want to make up my own mind about ...

It sometimes takes hours to dye my hair.

"I told you to take that gorilla to the zoo!"
"I took him to the zoo yesterday. I'm taking him to the beach today."

DISCUSSION

Are you sure you prefer to live in the country? There's nothing to do.

DISCUSSION STRATEGIES

Don't you think ...?
Is that why ...?
Are you sure ...?

Try to include the discussion strategies and the patterns from the controlled practice section in the following discussions.

What exciting or interesting things are there to do in big cities?
Do you think younger people or older people generally prefer big cities? Why?
Are people in the country mentally and physically healthier than people in the cities?
In the future, many cities will be much bigger than now. What problems will this cause?
How can more people be encouraged to live in country areas?
Is it important to keep up with the latest fashions and music? Why?
Is it OK to be materialistic sometimes?

Activities

FOLLOW-UP QUESTIONS

List three interesting places to visit in your area.

Examples: The art museum.
                  The beach.
                  The castle.

Now talk to another student and ask at least two follow-up questions about each point.

Examples:

A: How old is the castle?
B: I don't know, but maybe about
      three hundred years old.
A: Why is it interesting to visit?
B: It's not so famous, but there's a beautiful park
      around it, and there are many kinds of birds in
      the park.

ROLE PLAY

Student A: You are wondering where to take
                  a vacation.
Student B: Recommend one or two cities that
                  would be nice to visit (either in
                  your own country or a different
                  country).

Example questions:
What is there to see in London?
What shops do you recommend?

SITUATION - APOLOGIZING WITH REASONS

Brainstorming: *Think of good reasons to be late for school/work.*
                      Think of ways to say sorry.
                      Think of things you can do to make your boss happy.

Student A: *You live in a big city and have to commute to work. You are late for work six days in a row.*
                  Apologize to your boss and give reasons.

Examples:
I'm sorry I'm late. My alarm didn't go off
  and I overslept.
I apologize for being late again. I missed the train.
I'm extremely sorry for being late again.
  There was a big traffic jam.

Student B: *You are Student A's boss.*
                  You are not happy about the situation.

Examples:
You shouldn't go out late every night.
Did you oversleep again!
I thought you come by train!

"I'm sorry I'm late. I got married."
"Well make sure it doesn't happen again!"

6. City Life

Further Activities

COLLOCATION SETS

Put the following into sentences or dialogues:

City
1. a cosmopolitan city   *Example:*   New York and London are two of the most cosmopolitan cities I know.

2. an overcrowded city
3. an industrial city

Area
1. a convenient area   *Example:*   The area I live in is very convenient. I can go almost anywhere by bus or train.

2. a residential area
3. a farming area

Countryside
1. the surrounding countryside   *Example:*   It's easy to get out of the city, and some of the surrounding countryside is beautiful.

2. unspoiled countryside
3. picturesque countryside

SPEECHES

Prepare a short speech on one of these three topics:

All young people should live in big cities for a while.
The countryside is boring.
The growth of cities is leading to more loneliness and unhappiness.

EXTRA EXPRESSIONS

Put the following into short dialogues:

follow the crowd   a zebra crossing (British)
get stuck   a crosswalk (American)
                    We'll cross that bridge when we come to it.

Example:
A: What'll happen if we miss the last bus?
B: Let's cross that bridge when we come to it.

"There's a zebra crossing further down the street."
"I hope it's having better luck than I am."

Consolidation & Recycling

BUILDING VOCABULARY

Across

1   London and New York are very ___ cities.
7   There's a ___ view from my room.
8   I wish he would ___ more jokes.
9   My boss should understand that I'm ___.
10 All work and no ___ makes Jack a dull boy.
11 They showed up twenty minutes ___.
13 The ___ from factories and cars is terrible.
14 I work for the government. I'm a ___ servant.
16 It looks like you're ___ hard.
19 I'm ___ charge of my section.
20 We have a love-hate ___.

Down

1   How ___ you enjoy so much pain!
2   She's very ___. She loves being with people.
3   What's the ___ of Los Angeles?
4   The ___ restaurant near here is very good.
5   I live in a residential ___.
6   My relatives are scattered all over the ___.
10 I sit at my desk and do a lot of ___.
12 I go to work by ___.
14 Let's ___ that bridge when we come to it.
15 Which city would you like to ___?
17 I bumped ___ an old friend yesterday.
18 The city is ___ for my work.

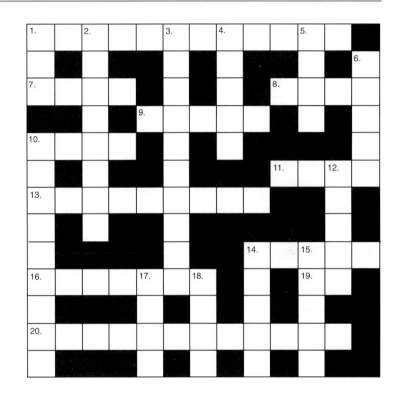

FOCUSING ON COLLOCATIONS

Write eight separate sentences, each of which includes both words in the pairs below:

large / population

best / friend

good / for

good / work

more / glamorous

old / fashioned

much / healthier

normal / for

WRITING OPINIONS

Write paragraphs about the following. Try to include words and patterns from this unit.

A city I know well.
My favorite place in the country.
The city I'd most like to live in.

REFLECTION

Which section of the unit did you find most interesting?
In which section of the unit did you learn the most?
Make a list of any new words and patterns from this unit that you want to try and remember.
You may find it helpful to write each word or pattern on a card.

7. Beliefs

WARM-UP QUESTIONS

Which numbers do you believe are lucky or unlucky?
What other things do you believe are lucky?
What other things do you believe are unlucky?
What interesting beliefs are common in your country?

VOCABULARY

Here are some words and expressions that will be useful in this unit.
How many do you know?

zodiac	fortune teller	vampires
ghosts	telepathy	superstition
supernatural	predict	interpret
character	astrology	cynical

Discuss which of the above words and expressions could fit in the following gaps.

Carlos: I went to see a _____ a few years ago, and she was able to _____ many things about my future. It's amazing that so much of what she said has come true.

Michelle: She probably said things that you could _____ in many different ways. So whatever she said would stand a good chance of coming true.

Carlos: You're being too _____. I'm sure she was genuine. Since then I've become very interested in studying the stars, so I read a lot about _____ and the _____. And I've also come to believe in _____ phenomena such as _____ and _____.

What words/phrases that are not in the list can you think of that might be useful when we talk about beliefs?

MIND MAP

Here is Carlos' mind map starting from 'beliefs'.

astrology — stars — zodiac

ghosts — supernatural — vampires

stars — beliefs

unlucky numbers — 13 — 4

supernatural

beliefs

love — first sight — lasts forever

Now make your own mind map with 'beliefs', 'fears', 'Zodiac signs' or 'blood types' in the center.
Talk about your mind map with another student or the rest of the class.

Fairytale: A True Story—Icon Productions

POINTS OF VIEW - WE CAN JUDGE A PERSON'S CHARACTER BY THEIR BLOOD TYPE

I think we can tell a lot about a person's character from their blood type. I've no idea how it works, but it seems to be pretty accurate. My blood type is O, and people who have O type blood are supposed to be individualistic and ambitious. I think it's true. I'm considered very individualistic in Japan, and I'm more ambitious than most people.

I don't believe a word of it! It's just superstition! Somebody probably made it all up, and made a lot of money out of it at the same time. My blood type is A. What am I supposed to be like?

You needn't be so cynical! Type A people are good at teamwork and usually cooperate with others. Type B people are unconventional and stand back from the world around them. Type AB are creative and good socializers, but often selfish at home.

I'm very bad at teamwork, even when I play soccer. My sister is Type B and she's the most conventional person I know, and one of my friends is AB and he's very unsociable and has never created a thing in his life. I don't know why so many people are taken in by this kind of nonsense.

7. Beliefs

Practice and Discussion

PERSONALIZATION

Complete these sentences with your own ideas.

We can tell a lot about a person's character from ...
I think ... is individualistic.
Some people consider me to be ...
I'm more ambitious than ...
I think ... are good at teamwork.
I've never ... in my life!
I don't know why so many people ...
I was once taken in by ...

Some people consider me to be too traditional.

"When is it unlucky to see a black cat?"
"When you're a mouse."

DISCUSSION

I'm not sure what love really is.

DISCUSSION STRATEGIES

I don't know why ...
I have no idea how ...
I'm not sure what ...

Try to include the discussion strategies and the patterns from the controlled practice section in the following discussions.

What's your blood type? Do you have the kind of character mentioned in *Points of View?*
If you know any of your family or friends' blood types, see how their characters compare.
Does reading your horoscope ever influence you?
Do you believe in ghosts? Why?
Do you believe in telepathy? Why?
Do you think some people can predict the future? Why?
Do you believe in love at first sight?

Activities

FOLLOW-UP QUESTIONS

List three unlucky things that some people believe in.

Examples: walking under a ladder
                  number 13
                  black cats

Now talk to another student and ask at least two follow-up questions about each point.

Examples:

A: Why do you think some people think it's unlucky to walk under a ladder?

B: Maybe something might fall on them.

A: Do you mind walking under ladders?

B: I'd probably walk around the ladder just to be careful.

ROLE PLAY

Student A: *You are a psychiatrist. Analyze Student B's dream.*

Student B: *Try to remember a real dream you have had, or invent a dream.*

Example questions:

Do you think there's any special reason why you dreamed about him?

What happened after that?

SITUATION - TRYING TO CONVINCE SOMEBODY THAT YOU'VE SEEN A GHOST

Brainstorming: *Think of times you may have seen a ghost.*
                       Think of stories you have heard of others' seeing a ghost.
                       Think of what a ghost might look like.

Student A: *Try to convince Student B that you have seen a ghost.*

Examples:

You'll never believe what I saw yesterday.

I'm telling the truth! I saw it sitting in front of the TV.

I'm not making this up! It even spoke to me.

Student B: *You don't believe Student A's story. Be cynical and ask questions about what happened.*

Examples:

I don't believe it! It must have been your imagination.

It was probably just somebody that looked like a ghost.

What did it say to you?

"I keep on imagining I'm a pair of curtains."
"Pull yourself together!"

7. Beliefs

Further Activities

COLLOCATION SETS

Put the following into sentences or dialogues:

Lucky
1. a lucky day
2. a lucky charm
3. third time's a charm

Example: It must be my lucky day! She said yes when I asked her for a date.

Luck
1. a stroke of luck

Example: We were losing the game, but suddenly had a stroke of luck— their best player was injured.

2. a bit of luck
3. beginner's luck

Believe
1. genuinely believe
2. firmly believe
3. deeply believe

Example: I'm being serious. I genuinely believe in vampires.

SPEECHES

Prepare a short speech on one of these three topics:

After we die we become ghosts.
All superstitions are imagination.
We can communicate with each other by telepathy.

EXTRA EXPRESSIONS

Put the following into short dialogues:

believe it or not
on the same wavelength
a skeleton in the closet

You look as if you've seen a ghost!

Example:
A: We're definitely on the same wavelength.
B: That's just what I was going to say.
A: Great minds think alike!

"Why did the skeleton stay in the closet while everybody else was having a party?"
"I've no idea."
"It had no body to dance with."

Consolidation & Recycling

BUILDING VOCABULARY

Across

1   I don't like it here, but the ___ countryside is beautiful.
5   I like people who forget my ___.
6   It would ___ a good chance of coming true.
8   Did you miss me ___ I was away?
9   Cities offer a chance to escape from a ____ life.
11   Better late than ___.
13   I don't believe in fortune ___.
14   It ___ as if it's going to rain.
16   My wife's brother is my brother ___ ___.
17   I might change my ___.
19   What are you doing ___ week?
20   I work ___ a large corporation.
21   Is there ___ space in the living room?

Down

1   I don't believe it! It's just a ___.
2   Not indoors.
3   Many people are taken in by this kind of ___.
4   They ___ me anything I wanted.
7   I'd like to ___ a happy home.
8   We are on the same ___. We have the same ideas.
10   She ___ me to be individualistic.
12   I'd go to a ___ above my garage.
15   I like to do a lot. I don't like to ___ time.
17   Waiter! What's on the ___ today?
18   I'm afraid of being laid ___.

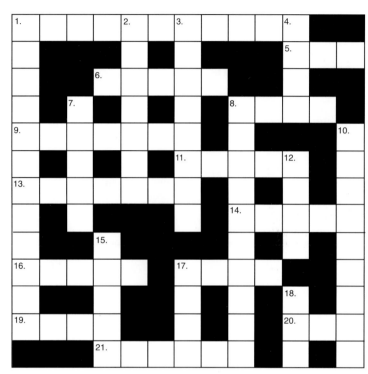

FOCUSING ON COLLOCATIONS

Write eight separate sentences, each of which includes both words in the pairs below:

am / considered   thinking / starting
takes / hours   deeply / believe
looks / like   same / wavelength
taken / in   take / after

WRITING OPINIONS

Write paragraphs about the following. Try to include words and patterns from this unit.

Zodiac signs and blood types.
Do ghosts exist?
My beliefs.

REFLECTION

Which section of the unit did you find most interesting?
In which section of the unit did you learn the most?
Make a list of any new words and patterns from this unit that you want to try and remember.
You may find it helpful to write each word or pattern on a card.

8. The Future

WARM-UP QUESTIONS

How do you think your life will be different ten years from now?
How do you think your country will be different ten years from now?
How do you think the world will be different ten years from now?
What would you love to do in the future?

VOCABULARY

Here are some words and expressions that will be useful in this unit.
How many do you know?

doubt	guess	probably
wonder	expect	unless
unpredictable	invent	by the time
discover	nobody knows	unlikely

Discuss which of the above words and expressions could fit in the following gaps.

Lee: I _____ what we will all be doing ten years from now. I _____ if I'll be living a very exciting life. I'll _____ be married and trying to earn enough money to support my family.

Hassan: _____ what's going to happen. The future is so _____. You might _____ something that will make you a fortune. You could be a millionaire _____ you are forty!

Lee: Not _____ I have an amazing stroke of luck! It's very _____ that anything like that will happen. I _____ I'll just be doing a normal nine-to-five job.

What words/phrases that are not in the list can you think of that might be useful when we talk about the future?

MIND MAP

Here is Lee's mind map starting from '100 years from now'.

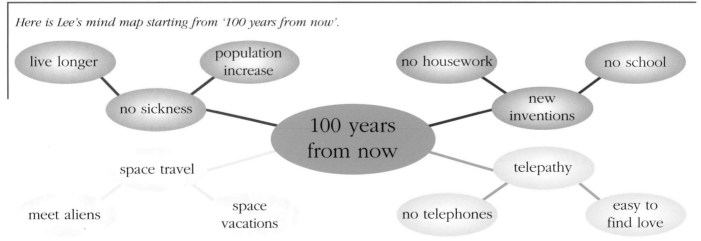

Now make your own mind map with '100 years from now', '10 years from now', 'next week' or 'next year' in the center.
Talk about your mind map with another student or the rest of the class.

Star Trek III: The Search for Spock—Paramount

POINTS OF VIEW - NOBODY WILL HAVE TO WORK

I predict that a hundred years from now hardly anybody will have to work because almost everything will be done by robots. We'll have much more leisure time! And scientists will have discovered how to keep people alive for hundreds of years.

If people live for hundreds of years, there'll be a terrible population problem. And if hardly anybody works, don't you think people will get very bored? That might lead to a lot of materialism and other social problems. It could mean crime would increase, too.

It's true that materialism may increase, but there will also be more time to have a richer and more cultured life. I don't think crime will increase. We'll learn more about what causes crime and be able to prevent it more effectively. Everybody will be much happier than now, doing whatever they like. There'll have to be some rules of course.

I guess the robots will enforce the rules! There'll be very few human police because hardly anybody will be working. We might even be governed by robots, too. It sounds like we could lose control of our own lives.

8. The Future

Practice and Discussion

PERSONALIZATION

Complete these sentences with your own ideas.

I predict that ...
Hardly anybody ...
Almost everything ...
100 years from now scientists will have discovered ...
If people live for hundreds of years ...
If hardly anybody works ...
In the future, we'll learn more about ...
In the future, we'll be able to prevent ...

> *Hardly anybody buys me birthday presents.*

"What am I going to be when I graduate from college?"
"An old man."

DISCUSSION

> *It might mean I could go to the beach every day!*

DISCUSSION STRATEGIES

That/it would/could/might lead to ...
That/it would/could/might mean ...
That/it would/could/might cause ...

Try to include the discussion strategies and the patterns from the controlled practice section in the following discussions.

Do you think people will work harder or less hard in the future? Why?
What do you think scientists will have discovered 100 years from now?
If people live longer, what effects will this have?
If people become more materialistic, what effects will this have?
Do you think humans will be living on other planets a hundred years from now? Why?
Would you like to live on another planet? Why?
If we do whatever we like, will we all be much happier?

Activities

FOLLOW-UP QUESTIONS

List three of your dreams for the future.

Examples: I'd love to travel around the world.
                I dream of living in a large house with
                   a beautiful garden.
                I want to be a famous actor.

*Now talk to another student and ask at least two
follow-up questions about each point.*

Examples:

A: Which places would you visit first?
B: Probably South America.
A: Why South America?
B: I want to watch soccer games in Brazil and
      Argentina.

ROLE PLAY

Student A: *You are a time traveler from the
                future explaining what's going to
                happen in the future.*
Student B: *Be yourself. Ask questions about
                the future.*

Example questions:
How long am I going to live?
Will there be another world war?

SITUATION - PROPOSING MARRIAGE

Brainstorming: *Think of good ways to ask somebody to marry you.*
                    Think of things you could promise.
                    How would you like to be asked?

Student A: *Ask B to marry you. Make promises
                about what you'll do if he/she accepts
                your proposal.*

Examples:

If you marry me, I'll do all the housework.
I promise I'll bring you breakfast in bed every day.
If you marry me, I'll be with you all the time.

Student B: *Consider whether to accept or not.*

Examples:

You say that now, but after we get married
   you'll forget what you said.
What kind of life do you think we'd have?
Do you mind if I have dates with other men/women?

"When we get married will you give me a ring?"
"Yes, of course. What's your telephone number?"

8. The Future

Further Activities

COLLOCATION SETS

Put the following into sentences or dialogues:

Future
1. a bright future
2. a future plan
3. worry about the future

Example: She's so talented. She has a very bright future ahead of her.

Dream
1. a wonderful dream

Example: Going to Hawaii was just like a wonderful dream. Now I have to face reality again.

2. the dream came true
3. achieve a dream

Hope
1. give up hope
2. a slight hope
3. the only hope

Example: I gave up hope. I knew he would never come back.

SPEECHES

Prepare a short speech on one of these three topics:

The world will destroy itself some time in the next fifty years.
Our descendants will marry aliens.
There will be a world government in the next fifty years.

EXTRA EXPRESSIONS

Put the following into short dialogues:

You never know.
Nothing is impossible.
Don't count your chickens
   before they're hatched.

Nobody can predict the
   future.

Example:
A: You don't seriously think the Dodgers will win?
B: You never know!

"Nothing is impossible."
"No, it isn't. I've been doing nothing for years."

Consolidation & Recycling

BUILDING VOCABULARY

Across

1 That might cause a serious social ___.
4 She has a great sense of ___.
7 We'll be able to prevent crime more ___.
9 Between you and ___.
10 I'm having dinner with a ___ from my office.
12 It's wonderful ___ be in good shape.
15 We could ___ control of our own lives.
18 If you marry me, I'll do all the ___.
20 I will ___ from college next year.
22 My house was redecorated last ___.
23 We've arranged a ___ to California.

Down

1 I ___ that humans will live on other planets in the future.
2 I work in a very busy ___.
3 I used to play on my ___ baseball team.
5 It's true that materialism ___ increase.
6 I like people who ___ my birthday.
8 In my ___ job, I'd travel a lot.
11 It's ___ that I'll become a millionaire.
13 I have a lot of energy to do ___ things as well.
14 It may ___ like I don't appreciate my parents.
16 I like to ___ in a hot bath.
17 Not traditional.
19 Did you miss me when I was ___?
21 The ___ is fresher in the country.

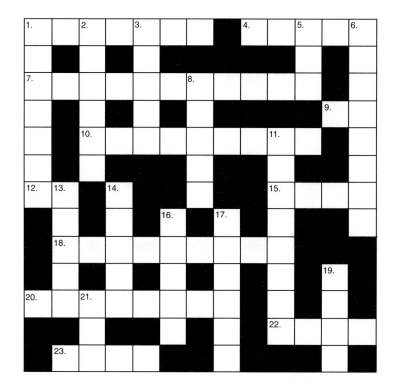

FOCUSING ON COLLOCATIONS

Write eight separate sentences, each of which includes both words in the pairs below:

dream / true
not / sure
probably / be
residential / area

doubt / if
time / off
become / scattered
might / lead

WRITING OPINIONS

Write paragraphs about the following. Try to include words and patterns from this unit.

Next month.
Ten years from now.
The future of the world.

REFLECTION

Which section of the unit did you find most interesting?
In which section of the unit did you learn the most?
Make a list of any new words and patterns from this unit that you want to try and remember.
You may find it helpful to write each word or pattern on a card.

9. Transportation

WARM-UP QUESTIONS

How do you usually get to work/school?
How is the transportation system in your area?
What do you usually do on the train or in a bus?
How do you feel about flying?

VOCABULARY

Here are some words and expressions that will be useful in this unit.
How many do you know?

break down	public transportation	stuck
get around	service	uncomfortable
fares	congested	irritated
punctual	dependent on	delayed

Discuss which of the above words and expressions could fit in the following gaps.

Sonchai: I'm thinking of getting a car. It will be much easier to _____. The _____ around here is not very reliable. The trains are often _____ because of the weather, and the buses aren't very _____.

Manosh: Yes, I don't know why the bus _____ is so bad. The _____ are very high, too, and the seats are often _____. But cars have problems as well. They sometimes ____, and once you get one, you'll always be _____ it.

Sonchai: I'll just use it when I have to, and when the roads are not too _____. I won't use it all the time.

What words/phrases that are not in the list can you think of that might be useful when we talk about transportation?

MIND MAP

Here is Sonchai's mind map starting from 'cars'.

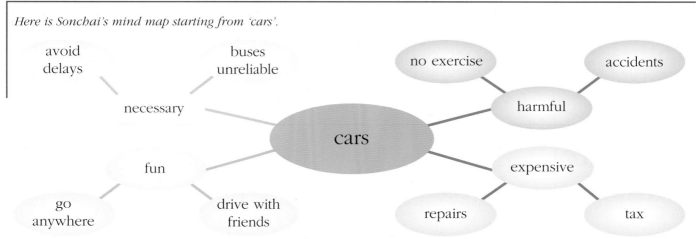

Now make your own mind map with 'cars', 'buses', 'trains' or 'camels' in the center.
Talk about your mind map with another student or the rest of the class.

Big Business—MGM

POINTS OF VIEW - DRIVING IS A GOOD WAY TO RELAX

I love driving! It's a great way to relax, and a good way to get rid of stress.

That's nonsense! Driving's one of the biggest causes of stress in our daily lives! Waiting at traffic lights or getting stuck in traffic jams makes people so irritated. I never drive to work any more. I always go by bicycle.

And breathe in all that dirty air? It's much healthier to go by car. Anyway, I'm not really talking about driving to work. I know that can be stressful sometimes. I'm talking about drives in the countryside. It's fantastic to drive to a beautiful place, and then get out and take a walk. People that say driving is unhealthy don't know what they're talking about.

You can't convince me that driving is healthy. Many people become too dependent on cars and don't do enough exercise. Cars also cause a lot of pollution and make the countryside ugly. There should be a much higher tax on all cars except those needed for genuine business purposes. That'd make cities nicer places to live in, and stop the countryside from being spoiled.

9. Transportation

Practice and Discussion

PERSONALIZATION

Complete these sentences with your own ideas.

... is a great way to relax.
... is a good way to get rid of stress.
... makes me irritated.
It's fantastic to ...
People that ... don't know what they're talking about.
Some people become too dependent on ...
I am too dependent on ...
I think there should be a higher tax on ...

People that smoke make me irritated!

"Did you know that somebody's killed in a traffic accident every two minutes?"
"He must get very tired of it."

DISCUSSION

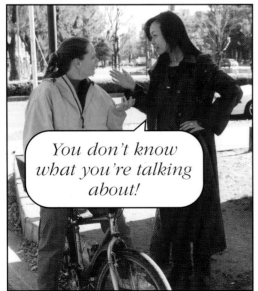

You don't know what you're talking about!

DISCUSSION STRATEGIES

You don't know what you're talking about!
That's nonsense!
That's ridiculous!

Try to include the discussion strategies and the patterns from the controlled practice section in the following discussions.

Is driving generally relaxing or tiring? Why do you think so?
Is it unhealthy to drive a lot?
Do you think cars should be banned from city centers? Why?
What kinds of transportation are absolutely necessary? Why?
What do you think will happen when the world's oil reserves get lower? Why?
What have been the good and bad effects of faster transportation?
What do you think will replace cars?

Activities

FOLLOW-UP QUESTIONS

List three ways the transportation system in your area could be improved.

Examples: There should be a monorail from
___ to ___.
The buses should have more
comfortable seats.
There should be more trains to ___.

*Now talk to another student and ask at least two
follow-up questions about each point.*

Examples:

A: Why do we need a new monorail line?
B: The roads are too congested.
A: Maybe there could be a special bus lane instead.
B: Monorails are much more comfortable
and faster than buses.

ROLE PLAY

Student A: You are very rich and have your
own private jet, submarine and
yacht.
Student B: Find out how Student A lives.

Example questions:
Where do you usually go in winter?
Why do you have a submarine?

SITUATION - STOPPED BY THE POLICE

Brainstorming: Think of things that can go wrong with a car.
Think of reasons you might be stopped by the police when driving.
Think of good excuses in each of these cases.

Student A: You are a highway police officer. You have stopped B for speeding, and you now find B doesn't have
a licence and there are many things wrong with B's car.

Examples:
One of your tires has a puncture.
How did you get those holes in the window?
Your lights don't seem to be working.

Student B: *Try to think of good excuses.*

Examples:
My lights were working last night.
  They must have just broken.
But I don't need brakes. I always drive slowly.
I don't need insurance. I've never had an accident.

"Pull over!"
"No, it's a pair of socks."

9. Transportation

Further Activities

COLLOCATION SETS

Put the following into sentences or dialogues:

Car
1. (My) car broke down.   *Example:*   Last week my parents' car broke down and we had to come home by taxi.

2. (My) car ran out of gas.
3. park (my) car

Traffic
1. a traffic jam   *Example:*   We were stuck in a traffic jam for hours.
2. heavy traffic
3. traffic lights

Train
1. miss the train   *Example:*   We were ten minutes late and missed the train.
2. catch the train
3. an express train

SPEECHES

Prepare a short speech on one of these three topics:

Local buses and trains should be free.
Bicycles are the best kind of transportation.
The faster the better.

EXTRA EXPRESSIONS

Put the following into short dialogues:

I don't know the first thing about ...

It's easy when you know how.

As soon as I hear the word ..., my mind goes blank.

Once you get used to it ...

Example:
A: What do you do when it breaks down?
B: I take it to a garage. I don't know the first thing about cars.

"How!"
"How!"
"I didn't know you could speak our language."
"It's easy when you know how."

Consolidation & Recycling

BUILDING VOCABULARY

Across

1   What she said came true. It was very ___.
5   I've no ___ how it works.
7   I ___ to work by monorail.
9   I want to ___ for a new job I saw in the paper.
10 When we get married will you give me a ___?
11 You ___ think differently after you get married.
13 I used to play on a basketball ___.
14 It would stop the countryside from ___ spoiled.
16 I love lying on the beach and getting a sun ___.
18 I believe in __. We can communicate without words.
20 Am I descended ___ a gorilla?
21 I want to ___ home and live by myself.
22 Not single.

Down

1   Somebody's killed in a traffic ___ every two minutes.
2   The seats aren't very ___.
3   Cities offer a chance to escape from a ___ life.
4   A boss should ___ males and females equally.
6   She likes to be the center of ___.
8   I like ___. I'm always comfortable in airplanes.
12 I ___ I could, but I can't.
15 It's very small. There's not much ___ in the living room.
17 There's a room ___ the garage.
18 I'll ___ you a story.
19 They stand back from the world around ___.
20 I asked ___ chicken, but this is duck.

FOCUSING ON COLLOCATIONS

Write eight separate sentences, each of which includes both words in the pairs below:

break / down
believe / in
traffic / jam
cosmopolitan / city

make / irritated
give / hope
dependent / on
prepared / to

WRITING OPINIONS

Write paragraphs about the following. Try to include words and patterns from this unit.

Cars.
Public transportation.
Transportation in the future.

REFLECTION

Which section of the unit did you find most interesting?
In which section of the unit did you learn the most?
Make a list of any new words and patterns from this unit that you want to try and remember.
You may find it helpful to write each word or pattern on a card.

10. Vices

WARM-UP QUESTIONS

What do you think about people who gamble?
What do you think about people who smoke?
What do you think about people who drink a lot?
What are your bad habits (vices)?

VOCABULARY

Here are some words and expressions that will be useful in this unit. How many do you know?

give up	cancer	drunk
alcoholics	addicted	heart attack
pregnant	willpower	passive smoking
hangover	depressed	legal

Discuss which of the above words and expressions could fit in the following gaps.

Karima: I can't stand people that get ___. Some people don't know when to stop drinking, and they think they are so clever and their opinions are so wonderful! All they get is a ___ the next day.

Carlos: I tried to ____ drinking once, and I almost succeeded. I'd become ___ to alcohol, and was scared of having a ____. Unfortunately, I lacked the ___ to completely stop.

Karima: I can understand people drinking too much when they are very ___ or having a lot of stress, but it's so unpleasant for other people around them. And a lot of people who drink too much end up as ____.

What words/phrases that are not in the list can you think of that might be useful when we talk about vices?

MIND MAP

Here is Karima's mind map starting from 'alcohol'.

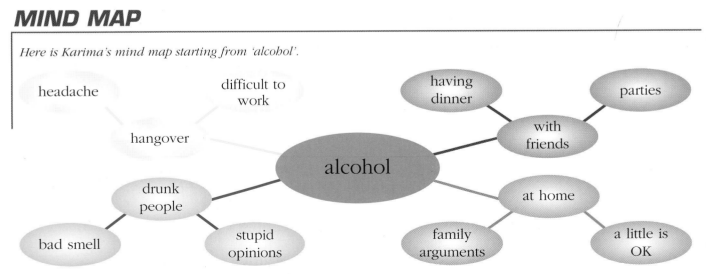

Now make your own mind map with 'alcohol', 'smoking', 'drugs' or 'bad habits' in the center.
Talk about your mind map with another student or the rest of the class.

Trainspotting—Figment/Noel gay/Channel 4, ph: Liam Longman

POINTS OF VIEW - SMOKING SHOULD BE MADE ILLEGAL

It's difficult for me to understand why smoking is still legal. It doesn't make sense to ban drugs like marijuana and not ban smoking, too. Smoking is just as addictive, just as dangerous and just as antisocial.

I don't agree. I enjoy smoking. We should be allowed to do a few things that are dangerous if we want to. It's natural that governments should ban most drugs, but they shouldn't take all the fun out of our lives.

The only reasons governments don't ban smoking are that they get so much money from the taxes on cigarettes and because the tobacco companies are too powerful. Millions of people are dying of cancer unnecessarily just so a few powerful companies can make a profit and governments can get more income.

I don't understand why you think there's some big conspiracy, and why I shouldn't be able to have a quiet smoke by myself if I want to. It's reasonable to have special smoking areas, discourage pregnant women from smoking, and make everyone aware of the dangers of passive smoking, but it's not necessary to make smoking illegal.

10. Vices

Practice and Discussion

PERSONALIZATION

Complete these sentences with your own ideas.

I think ... is addictive.
I think ... is antisocial.
I should be allowed to ... if I want to.
The only reason I ...
... is/are making a profit.
... as long as I ...
I'd like to make people more aware of ...
Governments should discourage ...

I'll pass my exam as long as I study hard.

"Coffee is addictive."
"Nonsense! I've been drinking coffee for years!"

DISCUSSION

It's hard for me to understand why I need to work so hard.

DISCUSSION STRATEGIES

It doesn't make sense to ...
It's difficult/hard/easy (for me) to understand/see why ...
I don't understand/see why ...

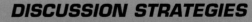

Try to include the discussion strategies and the patterns from the controlled practice section in the following discussions.

What things are you addicted to?
Do you think smoking is different from taking other drugs? Why?
What dangerous things do you do?
Should the government always try and prevent people from doing dangerous things?
What should be made illegal that is not illegal now? Why?
Do you think large businesses like the tobacco companies have too much power? Why?
To what extent should smokers respect the rights of non-smokers?

Activities

FOLLOW-UP QUESTIONS

List three things that can be addictive.

Examples: drinking coffee
                   playing computer games
                   gambling

*Now talk to another student and ask at least two
follow-up questions about each point.*

Examples:

A: Do you drink too much coffee?

B: No, but my father does. If he doesn't drink
        coffee, he can't work.

A: Why doesn't he try and sleep more, then he
        wouldn't need to drink so much?

B: It's too late. He's addicted.

ROLE PLAY

Student A: *You want to give up smoking.*
Student B: *You are a friend of Student A.*
                    Try hard to help him/her.

Example questions:
Have you tried chewing gum instead?
Do you know how bad it is for your health?

SITUATION - AT THE DOCTOR

Brainstorming: *Think of a medical problem each of you has.*
                       Think of how it affects you.
                       Think of various ways a doctor could treat it.

Student A: *You are a doctor giving Student B medical advice.*

Examples:
You should try and do more exercise.
How long have you been feeling like this?
Take these tablets three times a day, and come and
    see me next week.

Student B: *You are a patient with a problem.*

Examples:
I can't stop eating.
I wish I could find a way to feel less depressed.
I've tried everything I can think of,
    but nothing seems to work.

"Doctor! My hands won't stop shaking."
"Do you drink a lot?"
"No, I spill most of it."

10. Vices

Further Activities

COLLOCATION SETS

Put the following into sentences or dialogues:

Habit

1. an annoying/irritating habit   *Example:*   He has an annoying habit of always calling me just after I've gone to sleep.

2. a bad habit
3. make (it) a habit

Temptation

1. resist temptation   *Example:*   I needed to work, but I couldn't resist the temptation to play a computer game.

2. keep away from temptation
3. give in/way to temptation

Gamble

1. a big gamble   *Example:*   Playing with only two defenders was a big gamble.
2. the gamble failed
3. the gamble paid off

SPEECHES

Prepare a short speech on one of these three topics:

All cigarette and alcohol advertising should be banned.
People that smoke and drink too much are weak-willed.
Parents should never smoke at home.

EXTRA EXPRESSIONS

Put the following into short dialogues:

Do you mind if I ...?   I'd be very grateful if you
Would you mind not ...?   wouldn't ...
Is it all right if I ...?

Example:

A: Excuse me. Would you mind not smoking?
      This is a no-smoking area.
B: I'm sorry. I didn't see the sign.

"Do you mind if I cook dinner in my swim suit?"
"It'd be easier to use a saucepan."

Consolidation & Recycling

BUILDING VOCABULARY

Across

1   We need to be aware of the dangers of ___ smoking.
5   I'll bring you breakfast in ___ every day.
7   I don't care ___ I get married or not.
8   I have a ___ memory of going there years ago.
9   In the long ___.
10   ____ companies make a profit from cigarettes.
12   As ___ as I have a reasonable salary.
14   It will be ___ secure in the long run.
16   I'd like more ___ to have a more cultured life.
18   I have a badly-___ job.
19   He is always the ___ of attention.
20   Smoking should be banned. It should be ___.
21   Do you ___ if I sit here?

Down

1   Big corporations are too ___.
2   A ___ in the closet.
3   My hotel room had a beautiful ___.
4   The ___ around my house isn't good.
5   You've never played before! It's ___'s luck!
6   She ___ of living in a large house.
11   You don't need to be so ___!
13   When she sees an electronic ___, she wants to buy it.
15   I ___ enough money to support my family.
17   People that smoke make ___ irritated.
18   How can you enjoy so much ___!

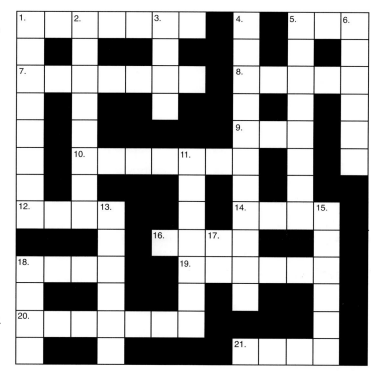

FOCUSING ON COLLOCATIONS

Write eight separate sentences, each of which includes both words in the pairs below:

give / up
worry / about
not / stand
not / enough

bad / habit
public / transportation
self / employed
make / aware

WRITING OPINIONS

Write paragraphs about the following. Try to include words and patterns from this unit.

The dangers of smoking.
Why do some people drink too much?
My vices.

REFLECTION

Which section of the unit did you find most interesting?
In which section of the unit did you learn the most?
Make a list of any new words and patterns from this unit that you want to try and remember.
You may find it helpful to write each word or pattern on a card.

11. Marriage

WARM-UP QUESTIONS

Do you think it is better to be married or single?
What do you think is the best age to get married?
How many children would you like to have? Why?
What things do you think make a successful marriage?

VOCABULARY

Here are some words and expressions that will be useful in this unit. How many do you know?

engaged	arranged	propose
anniversary	separate	wedding ceremony
divorce	opposite sex	affair
get to know	extravagant	single

Discuss which of the above words and expressions could fit in the following gaps.

Manosh: In my country, there are still a lot of marriages _____ between families. Even these days this can be a very good system for people that are shy or that don't have many chances to _____ members of the _____.

Michelle: I can understand how that system may have worked well in the past, but I think, nowadays, many young couples will soon ____ if their partners are decided by their families. Don't these kinds of marriages have high ___ rates?

Manosh: I doubt it. I know it's more romantic to think we should _____ to the one we love, get _____, then married, and live happily ever after. But, don't you think in love marriages, one or the other of the couple has unrealistic expectations, becomes disappointed, and may even be having an _____ before the second or third wedding _____! I think I'll stay _____!

What words/phrases that are not in the list can you think of that might be useful when we talk about marriage?

MIND MAP

Here is Manosh's mind map starting from 'marriage'.

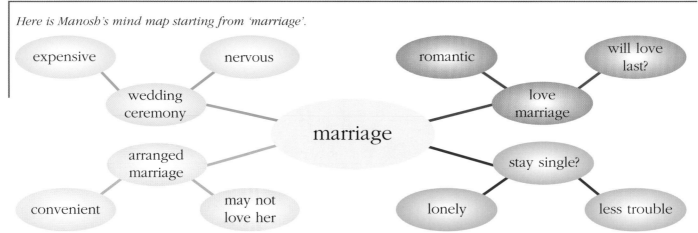

Now make your own mind map with 'marriage', 'people I'd like to date', 'weddings' or 'love' in the center.
Talk about your mind map with another student or the rest of the class.

Malcolm X—Warner brothers, ph: David Lee

POINTS OF VIEW - WEDDINGS SHOULDN'T BE EXTRAVAGANT

In some countries people spend ridiculous amounts of money on extravagant wedding ceremonies. They then spend even more on their honeymoons, new clothes, new furniture, and sometimes even a new house. It's crazy!

It's not as crazy as it seems. Most of those things are paid for by their parents. And those wedding ceremonies are special family gatherings. Anyway, don't you think it's natural for parents to want their children to start their new lives as happily and comfortably as possible?

No, I don't! When expensive things come too easily, we don't appreciate them. It's important for married couples to build their homes gradually by themselves. Their parents shouldn't spoil them by giving them so much.

The parents also want the couple to understand how important and special marriage is. They may think that if the wedding ceremony is too simple, the couple may divorce more easily. I think they have a strong argument. My impression is that divorce is less common in countries with traditional marriage ceremonies, but of course that may be for other reasons.

11. Marriage

Practice and Discussion

PERSONALIZATION

Complete these sentences with your own ideas.

Some people spend ridiculous amounts of money on ...
I think ...ing ... is extravagant.
It's natural for parents to ...
I sometimes don't appreciate ...
It's important for ...
Parents shouldn't spoil children by ...
I want ... to understand how ...
My impression is that divorce is ...

> It's natural for parents to love their children.

"Why is the bride wearing white?"
"Because white is the color of purity and happiness."
"Then why is the groom wearing black?"

DISCUSSION

> Finding a partner is not as easy as it seems.

DISCUSSION STRATEGIES

My impression is that ...
... is not as ... as it seems.
My guess is that ...

Try to include the discussion strategies and the patterns from the controlled practice section in the following discussions.

Describe your ideal partner.
What do you think of arranged marriages? Why?
What are the best ways to find a partner?
Do you think expensive weddings make anybody happier? Who? Why?
Why do you think the divorce rate is increasing?
Is it natural to have only one partner?
Why do people get married?

Activities

FOLLOW-UP QUESTIONS

List three good wedding presents.

Examples: a vase

                      toys

                      tea set

*Now talk to another student and ask at least two
follow-up questions about each point.*

Examples:

A: Why do you think it's a good idea to give toys?

B: Young parents are often short of money.

A: But they may not have children.

B: Well, if they have toys, it may encourage them
to have children.

ROLE PLAY

Student A: *Interview B about his/her ideal
wedding day.*

Student B: *You are getting married next
month and can choose any kind
of wedding celebrations you like.*

Example questions:

What kind of party would you like to have?

What would you like to wear during
   the ceremony?

SITUATION - HONEYMOONS

Brainstorming: *Think of ideal places to go to for a honeymoon.
Think of things you'd like to do.
Think of what could go wrong.*

Student A: *You are on your honeymoon with Student B. Suggest things to do.*

Examples:

Why don't we look around all the most fashionable stores?

Do you want to go on a roller coaster?

You're not much fun, are you? Maybe we're not suitable.

Student B: *You prefer to just have a quiet time together.*

Examples:

We could take a romantic walk.

It'd be nice to lie on the beach together.

You're not very romantic, are you?
  Maybe we're not suitable.

"Is it better to kiss with my eyes closed?"
"No, it's better to use your lips."

11. Marriage

Further Activities

COLLOCATION SETS

Put the following into sentences or dialogues:

Love
1. love forever   *Example:*   If you marry me, I'll love you forever.
2. fall in love
3. love with all my heart

Husband
1. a faithful husband   *Example:*   He's a very faithful husband. He never even considers having
                                         an affair.
2. future husband
3. a hen-pecked husband

Wife
1. a dominating wife   *Example:*   It's clear who's the boss. She's very much the dominating wife.
2. a suspicious wife
3. future wife

SPEECHES

Prepare a short speech on one of these three topics:

Marriage is unnecessary.
Same sex marriages should be just as accceptable as
     male-female marriages.
Love always dies.

EXTRA EXPRESSIONS

Put the following into short dialogues:

ask out   white wedding
take out   split up

Example:
A: I thought you two were going out together.
B: We split up last month.

*"She wanted a white wedding in her
grandmother's dress."*
"It must have been a beautiful wedding."
*"Yes, the wedding was fine but her
grandmother caught a terrible cold."*

Consolidation & Recycling

BUILDING VOCABULARY

Across

1 I don't want to divorce. I just want to ___.
5 I promise I'll ___ you breakfast in bed.
7 My parents both work to ___ our family.
9 I'd go to a ___ above my garage.
11 There's a store just ___ the corner.
12 I can't ___ getting up at five o'clock every day.
14 I think being self-employed ___ be more secure.
18 The city isn't special, but the ___ countryside is wonderful.
20 ___ time's a charm!
21 I believe in ___. We can predict the future from the stars.

Down

1 I'm always faithful but my wife is very ___ of me.
2 They are only interested in fashions and ___ music.
3 It's cool to be a bit ___.
4 They spend their time ___ electronic gadgets.
6 I'm ___ losing weight.
8 What is the best age ___ get married?
10 It ___ have worked well in the past.
13 He likes to ___ attention to himself.
15 If the ceremony is ___ simple, they may divorce easily.
16 People use cars too much, ___ ___ don't do enough exercise.
17 I love having ___ conversations with friends.
19 It's a good system for people who ___ shy.

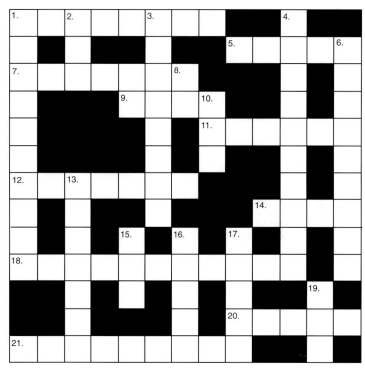

FOCUSING ON COLLOCATIONS

Write eight separate sentences, each of which includes both words in the pairs below:

get / know   it / natural
park / car   love / heart
become / disappointed   make / mind
hardly / anybody   should / allowed

WRITING OPINIONS

Write paragraphs about the following. Try to include words and patterns from this unit.

My ideal wedding day.
Love.
Being single.

REFLECTION

Which section of the unit did you find most interesting?
In which section of the unit did you learn the most?
Make a list of any new words and patterns from this unit that you want to try and remember.
You may find it helpful to write each word or pattern on a card.

12. Animals

WARM-UP QUESTIONS

What pets do you have or have you had in the past?
Can you name five animals that are in danger of becoming extinct?
Why do some people become vegetarians?
What animal would you most like to be?

VOCABULARY

Here are some words and expressions that will be useful in this unit.
How many do you know?

domestic	endangered	experiment
extinct	wild	survival of the fittest
evolution	mammals	species
reptiles	nature	dying out

Discuss which of the above words and expressions could fit in the following gaps.

Christina: Many _____ animals are now _____. The way things are going, there will be very few larger animals in the world except _____ ones like cows or sheep. It's very unnatural.

Lee: Maybe it's very natural! ___ is a basic law of _____, and Man has come out on top. We are the fittest! The other _____, and all the insects and _____ are simply not as good at surviving as we are.

Christina: That's a very cruel opinion. Many _____ are _____ and you just think it's natural! I suppose if aliens invade the earth and make Man ____, that will also be natural.

What words/phrases that are not in the list can you think of that might be useful when we talk about animals?

MIND MAP

Here is Christina's mind map starting from 'animals'.

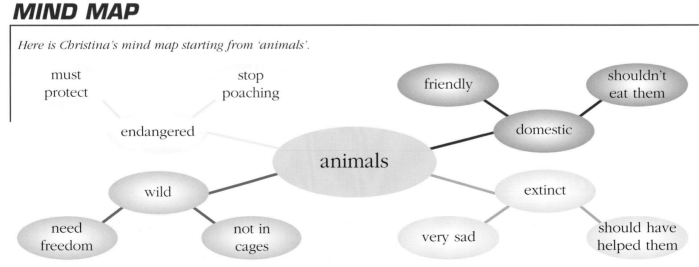

Now make your own mind map with 'animals', 'pets' or a particular animal (e.g. cows, dogs...) in the center.
Talk about your mind map with another student or the rest of the class.

K-9—Universal, ph: Marsha Blackburn

POINTS OF VIEW - THERE'S NO DIFFERENCE BETWEEN EATING COWS AND WHALES

I don't understand why so many people get upset if we eat some animals but not others. I realize that local customs and ways of looking at certain animals vary a lot, but it's not reasonable. We should either become vegetarians or accept that there is no difference between eating cows and eating whales.

I'm a vegetarian, and I think it's morally wrong to eat any kind of meat, but it's particularly wrong to eat the more intelligent species like whales. I think they must feel pain more than less intelligent species do. Anyway, surely it's wrong to eat any animal that's in danger of becoming extinct.

Yes, I accept that we shouldn't eat endangered species, but some types of whales are not on the endangered list. I'm also not sure whether intelligence should be the deciding factor. Should we condemn animals just because they are stupid?

There are experiments that show that plants have feelings, but most people accept that it's all right to eat plants. On the other hand, most of us would be horrified if somebody suggested eating a dog or a human. Perhaps it does come down to the level of intelligence of what we eat, or at least the degree of awareness of pain.

12. Animals

Practice and Discussion

PERSONALIZATION

Complete these sentences with your own ideas.

I get upset if ...
There is no difference between ...
I think it's morally wrong to ...
... are in danger of becoming extinct.
... are not on the endangered list.
There have been experiments that show ...
Most people accept that ...
Most people would be horrified if ...

> Most people accept that English is the international language.

"It's fantastic! Every time we ring this bell he gives us a piece of cheese. I think he might be intelligent!"

DISCUSSION

> I realize that animals have a right to live, but we need to kill them to survive. It's a cruel law of nature.

DISCUSSION STRATEGIES

I accept that ..., but ...
I admit that ..., but ...
I realize that ..., but ...

Try to include the discussion strategies and the patterns from the controlled practice section in the following discussions.

Is it better to eat cows than whales? Why?
Do you think we should all become vegetarians? Why?
Do you think we should conduct experiments on animals? Why?
How can we protect endangered species?
Do you think Man is an endangered species? Why?
If humans become extinct, which animal do you think will become dominant? Why?
Do you think plants have feelings? Why?

Activities

FOLLOW-UP QUESTIONS

List three pets you would like:

Examples: A dog
                A fish
                A horse

Now talk to another student and ask at least two follow-up questions about each point.

Examples:

A: What kind of dog would you like?
B: A dachshund. Whenever I see one, I smile.
A: I hear they can be noisy.
B: Yes, but they are very loyal and good with children.

ROLE PLAY

Student A: *You are a zoo administrator.*
Student B: *Interview Student A. You are wondering whether it is right to shut up animals in cages.*

Example questions:
How would you like to be shut up in a cage?
Why can't you at least give them more space to run around?

SITUATION - AT THE PET SHOP

Brainstorming: *Think of animals that are usually sold in pet shops.*
What other unusual animals could be pets?
Think of the problems of taking care of an unusual pet.

Student A: *You work in a pet shop. Help B find a pet.*

Examples:
How about a snake? They can protect your house very well.
You have to clean out the cage once every few days.
Have you thought about having a crocodile?

Student B: *You are looking for a pet. Ask about the good points and bad points of various pets and how to take care of them.*

Examples:
I'm looking for a quiet pet.
I'd like a pet that won't disturb the neighbors.
How do you take care of it?

"Do you know how long cows should be milked?"
"The same as short cows."

12. Animals

Further Activities

COLLOCATION SETS

Put the following into sentences or dialogues:

Animal

1. a carnivorous animal   *Example:*   Lions and tigers are carnivorous animals, and so am I.

2. a tame animal
3. behave like an animal

Fish

1. fish (around) for information/compliments   *Example:*   He works for another company, but he often comes in here fishing for information.

2. a fish out of water
3. There are plenty more fish in the sea.

Cat

1. Curiosity killed the cat.   *Example:*   If you ask, you may find out something you won't like. Curiosity killed the cat.

2. There isn't enough room to swing a cat.
3. When the cat's away the mice will play.

SPEECHES

Prepare a short speech on one of these three topics:

Humans and other animals are basically the same.
Pets are bad for children.
We should take care of animals less and humans more.

EXTRA EXPRESSIONS

Put the following into short dialogues:

As quiet as a mouse.   As blind as a bat.
The early bird catches the   Straight from the horse's
  worm.   mouth.

Example:

A: He never wakes me up. He's always as quiet as a mouse when he comes home late.

B: So you don't know what time he gets home!

"You're as blind as a bat!
Have your eyes ever been checked?"
"No, they've always been blue."

Consolidation & Recycling

BUILDING VOCABULARY

Across
1   Some types of whales are not on the ___ list.
7   I feel ___ for people who go to big cities.
8   You're living in the ___!
9   He's behaving like an ___.
10 Let's ___ that bridge when we come to it.
11 ___ is morally wrong to eat meat.
13 Maybe aliens will invade the ___.
15 There should be a no-smoking ___.
17 We are on the ___ wavelength.
20 My family are ___ all over the place.
22 Many ___ are dying out.
23 Many people get ___ if we eat whales.

Down
1   In love, we often have unrealistic ___.
2   Scientists will ___ how to travel to other galaxies.
3   When things come too ___, we don't appreciate them.
4   I'd like to ___ from my routine life.
5   How ___ you take care of it?
6   Large corporations try to make a ___.
9   I'd like to ___ him out for a date.
12 I'd like a pet ___ doesn't bite.
14 We'll be able to stay ___ for hundreds of years.
16 The early bird ___ the worm.
18 If you smoke too much, you'll have a ___ attack.
19 I think they must ___ a lot of pain.
21 My ___ to Europe was canceled.

FOCUSING ON COLLOCATIONS

Write eight separate sentences, each of which includes both words in the pairs below:

get / upset
fall / love
in / danger
whatever / like

disturb / neighbors
millions / people
way / relax
fish / water

WRITING OPINIONS

Write paragraphs about the following. Try to include words and patterns from this unit.

A pet I would like to have.
An animal I would like to be.
Vegetarianism.

REFLECTION

Which section of the unit did you find most interesting?
In which section of the unit did you learn the most?
Make a list of any new words and patterns from this unit that you want to try and remember.
You may find it helpful to write each word or pattern on a card.

13. Computers

WARM-UP QUESTIONS

How often do you use a computer?
What do you use a computer for?
What kind of computer would you like to have?
What is your favorite computer game?

VOCABULARY

*Here are some words and expressions that will be useful in this unit.
How many do you know?*

on-line	install	modem
download	access	security
CD-ROM	network	virus
attachment	interactive	delete

Discuss which of the above words and expressions could fit in the following gaps.

Manosh: Somebody sent me an _____ the other day and it infected my computer. I've _____ the file that caused the problem and it didn't do too much damage, but I think I'd better _____ some anti-_____ software.

Sonchai: It's easy to do. You can _____ the software from the Internet or use a _____. It's also worth improving the general _____ of your computer, especially if it is part of a _____ or if it is permanently _____. You don't need to worry so much if you dial up using a _____, but that's much less convenient.

Manosh: Yes. I've heard all kinds of people may try and get _____ to my computer if I'm not careful. I don't know why! I don't keep anything important on it.

What words/phrases that are not in the list can you think of that might be useful when we talk about computers?

MIND MAP

Here is Manosh's mind map starting from 'computers'.

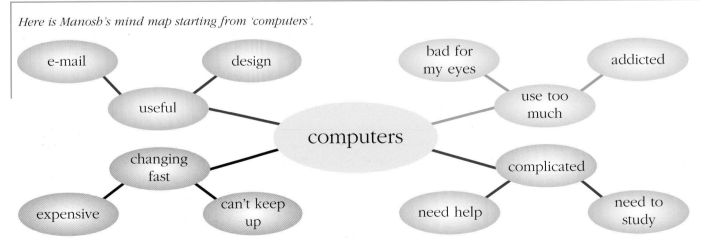

*Now make your own mind map with 'computers', 'mobile telephones', 'television' or 'new technology' in the center.
Talk about your mind map with another student or the rest of the class.*

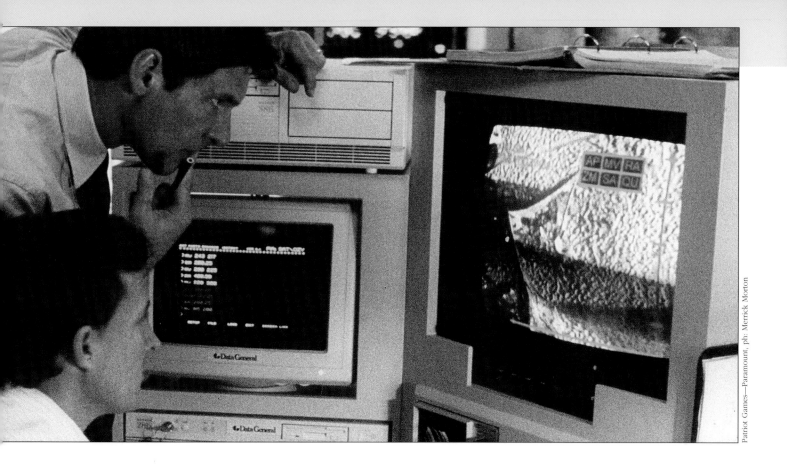

Patriot Games—Paramount, ph: Merrick Morton

POINTS OF VIEW - COMPUTER GAMES ARE BAD FOR CHILDREN

I know children who play computer games all the time. It can't be very good for them. They're in a world of their own. They don't go outside, and they don't know how to relate to other people.

It sounds like they're having a good time! And learning a lot at the same time. A child can learn so much by playing, solving puzzles and getting better at something. And computer games can keep children's attention for such long periods of time. It must help their ability to concentrate and keep working at things.

Children need to run around and play with each other. They shouldn't just sit in front of their computer screens. It must be bad for their eyesight, too. I hate to think what all these children will be like when they grow up. They'll be so unsociable!

I expect they'll be pretty good at handling all the new technology that is being developed. They'll be more curious about things as well. Anyway, how much time did we used to spend watching TV? Our parents thought we'd all become dull and passive. Perhaps they were right, and interactive computer games could be the way of making sure it doesn't happen to the next generation.

13. Computers

Practice and Discussion

PERSONALIZATION

Complete these sentences with your own ideas.

... isn't very good for me.
When I ... I'm in a world of my own.
I don't know how to ...
I'm getting better at ...
... helps me concentrate.
... is bad for our eyesight.
I'm curious about ...
My parents think/thought I ...

I don't know how to drive.

"The battery's flat."
"What shape is it supposed to be?"

DISCUSSION

It must be bad for me to eat so much ice cream.

DISCUSSION STRATEGIES

It should be ...
It must be ...
It can't be ...

Try to include the discussion strategies and the patterns from the controlled practice section in the following discussions.

Do/did you play a lot of computer games?
How will children in the future be different from children now? Why?
Do you think the best way for children to learn is through playing games? Why?
How can computers be used more in education?
How do you think computers will develop in the future?
Are computers having any harmful effects on society?
What are the main benefits of computers?

Activities

FOLLOW-UP QUESTIONS

List three ways computers can be helpful:

Examples: For designing posters.
               For sending e-mails to friends.
               For storing information.

*Now talk to another student and ask at least two
follow-up questions about each point.*

Examples:

A: Are you good at designing posters?
B: Not so good, but I enjoy it, and it's much easier
      on a computer.
A: Why is it easier?
B: Drawing lines and shapes or adding color is
      almost automatic, and I can paste pictures or
      photographs.

ROLE PLAY

Student A: *You are showing Student B how
                to use a computer.*
Student B: *You don't know anything about
                computers.*

Example questions:
What do I do after that?
How can I draw pictures?

SITUATION - AT A COMPUTER STORE

Brainstorming: *Think of hardware you can buy in a computer store.*
                    Think of software you can buy in a computer store.
                    Think of computer accessories you can buy.

Student A: *You want to sell Student B as many things as possible. Explain why he needs each item.*

Examples:
You definitely need a very large monitor.
This is one of my favorite games.
   I definitely recommend it.
How about having a virtual pet in the
   computer?

Student B: *You have a lot of money
                and want to buy a
                computer, software and
                computer accessories.
                Discuss what to buy with
                Student A.*

Examples:
Which computer's best for graphic
   design?
What kind of printer should I get?
I'm looking for some good games.

"I just repaired Santa Claus' computer."
"Really!"
"Yes! He said to me, 'If you're a computer expert, then I'm Santa Claus.'"

13. Computers

Further Activities

COLLOCATION SETS

Put the following into sentences or dialogues:

Computer
1. the computer is down
2. a laptop computer
3. computer graphics

Example: All the computers at school are down for some reason.

Technology
1. the latest technology
2. Information Technology
3. advanced technology

Example: My new computer uses all the latest technology.

E-mail
1. access e-mail
2. receive e-mail
3. check e-mail

Example: I haven't been able to access my e-mail for a few days.

SPEECHES

Prepare a short speech on one of these three topics:

Computers will take over the world.
The electronic age has taken the romance out of life.
We will all be able to work from home in the future.

EXTRA EXPRESSIONS

Put the following into short dialogues:

cut my/your work in half	wishful thinking
doesn't work	drive me crazy

Example:

A: Have you heard? Our new computers are going to make our work much easier.
B: That's just wishful thinking.

"This computer will cut your work in half!"
"In that case, I'll take two."

Consolidation & Recycling

BUILDING VOCABULARY

Across

1   Many people may try to get ___ to your computer.
4   I need to ___ the file that has the virus.
7   Domestic animals are usually ___.
8   I wish I'd been more interested in ___ and history.
10 For many people there's no ___.
12 Do ___ think plants have feelings?
13 Be careful! You might have a heart ___!
14 They are ___ not as good at surviving.
17 There are less jobs in country ___.
18 They'll be good at handling all the new ___.
20 I never drive to work ___ more.
21 A ___ doesn't eat meat.

Down

1   Don't open the ___ that came with the e-mail.
2   Divorce is less ___ in some countries than others.
3   Don't tell anybody! It's a ___!
5   Many species have become ___.
6   The ___ bird catches the worm.
9   ___ killed the cat.
11 My pets help me ___ down.
14 Being self-employed will be more ___.
15 My company can't make a ___.
16 Do you ___ to keep in good shape?
17 I like people that forget my ___.
19 ___ is the fittest animal!

FOCUSING ON COLLOCATIONS

Write eight separate sentences, each of which includes both words in the pairs below:

send / e-mail
get / rid
definitely / recommend
learn / more

helps / me
only / reason
lucky / day
kinds / people

WRITING OPINIONS

Write paragraphs about the following. Try to include words and patterns from this unit.

What I use a computer for.
The effect of computers on children.
How have computers changed society?

REFLECTION

Which section of the unit did you find most interesting?
In which section of the unit did you learn the most?
Make a list of any new words and patterns from this unit that you want to try and remember.
You may find it helpful to write each word or pattern on a card.

14. The Generation Gap

WARM-UP QUESTIONS

What kind of music do you like? Why?

Do you like wearing fashionable clothes? Why?

Do you feel young or old? Why?

In which ways are twenty-year-olds usually different from fifty-year-olds?

VOCABULARY

Here are some words and expressions that will be useful in this unit. How many do you know?

argue	criticize	rebel
find fault	conservative	immature
radical	conform	qualification
adolescent	settle down	adult

Discuss which of the above words and expressions could fit in the following gaps.

Jin-Sook: Why is it that older people are so often more ___ than younger people? And why do so many older people treat us as if we were _____ children?

Michelle: I know what you mean. My parents ___ in almost everything I do, so we always ____. They completely misunderstand me. I'm not a _____. I'm not even an ____ any more. I'm a mature _____ with my own opinions, that just happen to be different from theirs.

Jin-Sook: Our ideas may sometimes seem too _____, so I understand why older people _____ us, but we have a right to live our own lives and make our own mistakes. I know they do it because they love us, but ...

What words/phrases that are not in the list can you think of that might be useful when we talk about the generation gap?

MIND MAP

Here is Jin-Sook's mind map starting from 'the older generation'.

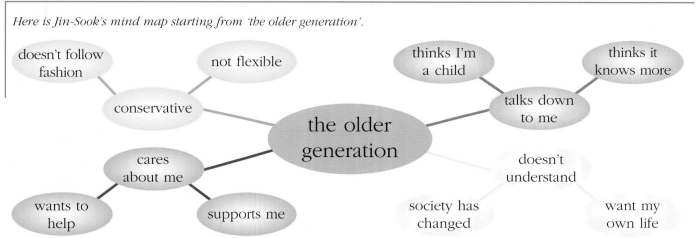

Now make your own mind map with 'the older generation', 'the young generation', 'family arguments', 'independence' in the center. Talk about your mind map with another student or the rest of the class.

Bus Stop—20th Century Fox

POINTS OF VIEW - YOUNG PEOPLE SHOULD GET STEADY JOBS

Why don't you get a steady job and a normal hair cut? Sooner or later you're going to have to get some qualifications, find a good job, and settle down.

I don't need those kinds of things. I want to be with people that are creative and artistic, and who aren't afraid to be different. I get bored when I'm with people that do the same thing every day or just want to be like everybody else. I think it's important for each of us to be ourselves and not just follow the crowd.

There's no need to lose your individuality. There are a lot of people that have steady jobs and follow society's rules, but who question those rules and try to improve them. People like that are more effective in changing society. They may seem to do the same thing every day, but they are gradually gaining the experience and power to improve things.

By the time they have enough power they are too old. When people get older they become more conservative and don't want to make changes any more. It's young people that have new ideas, but if we get regular jobs the managers don't listen to what we have to say. There's no point in conforming. It doesn't get us anywhere.

Practice and Discussion

PERSONALIZATION

Complete these sentences with your own ideas.

Sooner or later I'm going to ...
I want to be with people that ...
I think ... aren't/isn't afraid to be different.
I get bored when ...
I think ... follow(s) the crowd too much.
I question ...
I'm gradually ...
... doesn't get me anywhere.

I'm gradually losing weight.

"I've spent six years at university taking medicine."
"I hope you're feeling a little better now."

DISCUSSION

There's no point in working hard.

DISCUSSION STRATEGIES

There's no reason to ...
There's no need to ...
There's no point in ...

Try to include the discussion strategies and the patterns from the controlled practice section in the following discussions.

Do you think older people tend to be conservative? For example?
At what age should young people be treated as adults by their parents? Why?
Do you think young people should be given more power to change things? Why?
Do you think younger people or older people follow the crowd more?
   For example?
How can we improve mutual understanding between the generations?
Have you ever thought of dropping out? Why?
Do you tend to look at people younger than you as immature and childish?

Activities

FOLLOW-UP QUESTIONS

List three differences between the life of a student and the life of an office worker:

Examples: A student has more vacations.
A student studies more.
Parents support students more.

Now talk to another student and ask at least two follow-up questions about each point.

Examples:

A: If you worked in an office, would you also study?
B: Yes, I'd probably study English in the evening.
A: Would you study a lot?
B: Not so much. Just once or twice a week.

ROLE PLAY

Student A: *You are interviewing Student B.*
Student B: *You are wondering whether to continue working in an office or going to study overseas.*

Example questions:
How will you pay for everything?
If you continue working, will you get a better position in the future?

SITUATION - COMPARING THE PAST WITH THE PRESENT

Brainstorming: *Think of how life was different 30-40 years ago.*
Think what young people did in their free time.
Think what the fashions may have been like.

Student A: *You are old. Try to convince B that life was much better when you were young.*

Examples:
When I was young everything was much cheaper.
We used to go swimming in that river but it's much too dirty now.
Our teachers were stricter, but we had a much better education.

Student B: *You are young. You are interested in A's past, but you have doubts about A's opinions.*

Examples:
In which ways was education better?
Wasn't it more difficult to travel to other countries in those days?
What stores and restaurants did you go to?

"When I was your age, I thought nothing of going for a run every morning."
"I don't think much of it, either."

14. The Generation Gap

Further Activities

COLLOCATION SETS

Put the following into sentences or dialogues:

Generation

1. future generation(s) *Example:* If we don't protect the forests, future generations will have a lot of problems.

2. the younger generation
3. the generation gap

Age

1. look (one's) age *Example:* I would have guessed she was much younger. She doesn't look her age.

2. act (one's) age
3. a difficult age

Fashion

1. go out of fashion *Example:* Short skirts will soon go out of fashion.
2. a fashion magazine
3. the latest fashion

SPEECHES

Prepare a short speech on one of these three topics:

Young people are not individualistic enough. Too many of them follow the same fashions and listen to the same music.

Young people should respect old people and follow their advice.

People should try everything possible to keep themselves mentally young.

EXTRA EXPRESSIONS

Put the following into short dialogues:

two wrongs don't make a right
sit on the fence

getting somewhere/nowhere
bang your head against a brick wall.

Example:

A: There's no point in trying to persuade him. He never listens to a word we say.

B: Yes, I know. We'd only be banging our heads against a brick wall.

"We're getting nowhere! Let's compromise. If you agree that I'm right, I'll agree that you're wrong."

Consolidation & Recycling

BUILDING VOCABULARY

Across

1 I trust her predictions. I'm sure she was ___.
4 They treat us ___ if we were children.
7 I know what you ___.
8 Some people don't know when to ___.
10 She drives ___ crazy.
11 It's a ___. So we have to follow it.
13 It doesn't get us ___.
15 IT - ___ Technology.
18 I want to be with people that are ___ and artistic.
20 I know we ___ our parents a lot.
21 We disagree a lot, so we always ___ with each other.
22 Driving is a good way to get rid of ___.

Down

1 The younger ___ doesn't have enough experience to understand.
2 There's a gym ___. In fact, it's just around the corner.
3 It's a basic law of ___.
5 I worked in a ___ town.
6 Playing computer games is more ___ than watching TV.
9 A father or mother.
12 I don't ___ want to talk to anybody.
14 I got it straight from the ___'s mouth.
16 It shouldn't be the deciding ___.
17 You might ___ something that will make you a fortune.
19 We'll be ___ to prevent crime.
20 We're ___ big happy family.

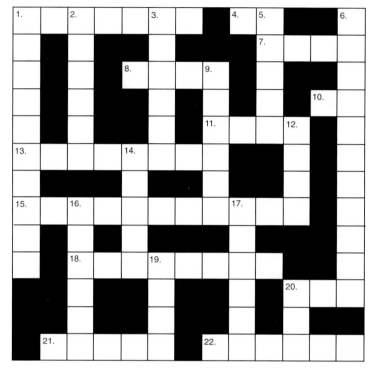

FOCUSING ON COLLOCATIONS

Write eight separate sentences, each of which includes both words in the pairs below:

steady / job
bad / eyesight
look / age
not / reliable

get / anywhere
most / accept
gradually / getting
predict / that

WRITING OPINIONS

Write paragraphs about the following. Try to include words and patterns from this unit.

Modern fashion.
The latest music.
How the generation gap has affected me.

REFLECTION

Which section of the unit did you find most interesting?
In which section of the unit did you learn the most?
Make a list of any new words and patterns from this unit that you want to try and remember.
You may find it helpful to write each word or pattern on a card.

15. Travel

WARM-UP QUESTIONS

What's the best place you've ever been? Why?
Where would you like to go for your ideal vacation? Why?
Do you prefer to travel by yourself or with a group? Why?
List five reasons why people like to travel.

VOCABULARY

Here are some words and expressions that will be useful in this unit.
How many do you know?

souvenirs	currency	discount ticket
abroad	package tour	exchange rate
travel agency	get lost	jet lag
sunbathe	insurance	out-of-the-way

Discuss which of the above words and expressions could fit in the following gaps.

Michelle: I go ____ a lot, and it doesn't usually cost very much. I can get a ____ from the ____, I don't stay in expensive hotels, I don't buy many ____, and each trip is short so I don't take out any ____. Of course, the total cost depends on the ____. If the local ____ is strong, it can be very expensive.

Hassan: I don't like to travel so much, and I always suffer from ____ for the first few days, so if I go anywhere, I like to take long trips, and usually to ____ places.

Michelle: I'd ____ if I went to places like that, and I prefer to take short trips just to change my feeling. I often go to an island for a few days and just ____ on the beach.

What words/phrases that are not in the list can you think of that might be useful when we talk about travel?

MIND MAP

Here is Michelle's mind map starting from 'travel'.

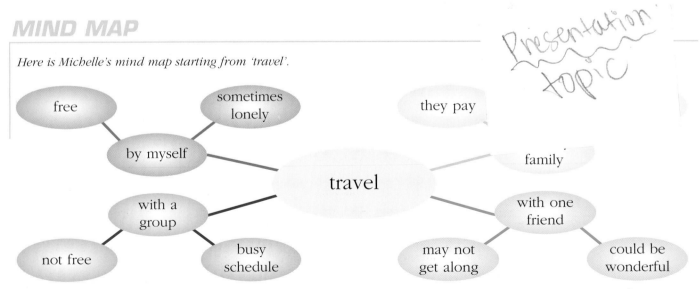

Now make your own mind map with 'travel', 'vacations', 'countries I want to visit', or 'cities I want to visit' in the center.
Talk about your mind map with another student or the rest of the class.

POINTS OF VIEW - I USUALLY JOIN A TOUR GROUP

I have a ten-day vacation every summer. I love visiting other countries and seeing the famous sights of London, Rio de Janeiro, Bangkok, Paris ... It's so exciting! I can make a lot of new friends, too. I usually join a tour group and we do everything together.

I can't travel like that. For me, looking at famous sights is no different from watching them on TV. It's often said that travel broadens the mind, but I don't think that's always true. When we travel we have to make an effort to get to know local people, and share experiences with them. That's why I prefer to visit country areas and stay in small family hotels.

I don't think you are being reasonable. I doubt if many people get long enough vacations to do that kind of thing. I only get ten days vacation a year! And anyway, I think there's a lot we can understand about a culture from visiting museums and art galleries, or listening to tour guides. And I don't have enough confidence to go off into the countryside on my own.

Why don't you try a short adventure holiday? You can still stay with a group of people, though they would be from various countries instead of just from your own country, and you could go hiking or cycling together. I bet that after you get away from the famous tourist sights once, you'll never want to go back.

15. Travel

Practice and Discussion

Complete these sentences with your own ideas.

I'd make a lot of new friends if I ...
It's often said that ...
I have to make an effort to ...
I want to get to know ...
I'd like to share ...
I don't have enough confidence to ...
I'd like to try ...
After I ... once, I might never ...

> I'd like to share an apartment with Tomoko.

"Did you have any trouble with your French when you were in France?"
"No, but French people did."

> I bet it'll rain every day if I take a vacation. It always does!

DISCUSSION STRATEGIES

I bet ...
I doubt if ...
I guess ...

Try to include the discussion strategies and the patterns from the controlled practice section in the following discussions.

What do you like doing when you travel?
Talk about places you have visited.
How do you feel about traveling by yourself?
If you had six month's vacation, what would you do?
Do you think travel broadens the mind? Why?
What are the best ways to get to know local people when you travel?
What places would you recommend a visitor to go to in your country? Why?

Activities

List three places you would like to go.

Examples: Hawaii
                 London
                 Egypt

Now talk to another student and ask at least two follow-up questions about each place.

Examples:

A: What would you do in Hawaii?
B: I'd go to the beach every day.
A: Do you like water sports?
B: No, I just like to relax on the beach and swim a bit.

Student A: You are a travel agent. Try to persuade B to go to very unusual places, giving lots of reasons.

Student B: You are at a travel agency choosing where to go for a vacation. Reject A's suggestions and give reasons.

Examples:

How about the Sahara Desert?
   It's very nice at this time of the year.
Why are you worrying so much?
   It's only dangerous after sunset.

- GIVING A GUIDED TOUR

Brainstorming: *Think of the nicest places to visit in your area.*
                         Think of things that happened in your area in the past.
                         Think of famous people who came from or lived in your area.

Student A: You are a tour guide. Imagine you are showing B around the local area or another place you are familiar with. Explain about local places of interest.

Examples:

This is where one of our most famous poets lived.
If we climb up that hill, we'll have a beautiful view of the bay.
This temple was built about eight hundred years ago.

Student B: You are a tourist. Ask A questions about the various places he/she shows you.

Examples:

Could you tell me a little about the castle's history?
Why was he famous?
Are there any good art galleries or museums in the area?

"What do you think of that new restaurant on Mars?"
"The food's good, but there isn't much atmosphere."

15. Travel

Further Activities

COLLOCATION SETS

Put the following into sentences or dialogues:

Vacation

1. family vacation	*Example:*	We always go to the same place for our family vacation.
2. annual vacation		
3. on vacation		

Flight

1. non-stop flight	*Example:*	It's a non-stop flight to Washington.
2. a comfortable flight		
3. miss the flight		

Tourist

1. a tourist attraction	*Example:*	The aquarium is one of the main local tourist attractions.
2. tourist information		
3. a tourist destination		

SPEECHES

Prepare a short speech on one of these three topics:

Taking vacations abroad is a waste of money.
If everybody traveled more, there wouldn't be any more wars.
Traveling is more tiring than staying at home.

EXTRA EXPRESSIONS

Put the following into short dialogues:

it's a small world   get away
peace and quiet   have the time of your life

Example:

A: That's an incredible coincidence! I lived there when
       I was a child, too.
B: It's a small world!

*"We'll soon be relaxing on an exotic beach,
soaking up the sun, having the time of our lives."
"Yes, but it's a pity I didn't bring my overcoat."
"It'll be over 40°c. You don't need an overcoat!"
"Yes, I do. The tickets are in one of the pockets."*

Consolidation & Recycling

Across

1   Paris is a popular tourist ___.
7   I've seen a ___. He looked like Dracula.
9   Nothing ___ to work.
10   They don't know how to ___ to other people.
11   I usually ___ on the fence.
12   I'll pass my ___ as long as I study hard.
13   Driving is a good way to ___.
17   What are you doing this ___?
18   I need to take some time ___ work.
20   Why do you ___ there's a big conspiracy?
21   I dream of ___ in a large house.
23   If you need a map, go to the ___ information office.

Down

1   I think we should either ___ or separate.
2   We are ___. We both like doing the same things.
3   I live in a residential ___.
4   I never get sick, so I don't take out any ___.
5   She ___ more excitement in her life.
6   People get ___ if we eat some animals but not others.
8   It's wrong to eat the more ___ species.
12   There will be few large animals left ___ domestic ones.
14   I don't like looking at famous ___.
15   I usually buy a discount ___.
16   It's a small ___.
19   I do a nine-to-___ office job.
22   Do you want to ___ hiking?

Write eight separate sentences, each of which includes both words in the pairs below:

have / confidence   tourist / attraction
get / bored   endangered / list
change / feeling   often / said
not / crazy   nobody / knows

Write paragraphs about the following. Try to include words and patterns from this unit.

A trip/vacation I remember well.
A country I'd like to visit.
Is travel important?

Which section of the unit did you find most interesting?
In which section of the unit did you learn the most?
Make a list of any new words and patterns from this unit that you want to try and remember.
You may find it helpful to write each word or pattern on a card.

Featured Movies

Bowfinger *(pg. 8)*
(1999) Universal Pictures
Steve Martin, Eddie Murphy, Heather Graham
Director: Frank Oz

A comedy, in which failed filmmaker Bobby Bowfinger (Martin) decides to revive his fortunes by making his accountant's screenplay about aliens invading in raindrops. His only problem is his intended megastar, Kit Ramsey (Murphy), is paranoid and refuses to take part. To overcome this problem Bowfinger hits on an ingenious and hilarious plan – to film his leading man without his knowledge.

The Endless Summer II *(pg. 14)*
(1994) New Line Cinema
Director: Bruce Brown

Bruce Brown became a cult hero in 1966 when he directed the hit surfing documentary *The Endless Summer*. Twenty-eight years later, with a bigger budget, he took two young surfers and made an even more spectacular sequel. Stunning, unspoilt beaches, and unusual locations made *The Endless Summer II* a feast for the eyes and the senses. Not just for surfers!

The Little Rascals *(pg. 20)*
(1994) Amblin
Director: Penelope Spheeris

A slapstick comedy about a gang of children and their adventures, based on the great Hal Roach's *Our Gang* comedy series from the 1920's. Spanky and the members of the He-Man Women Haters Club find out that gang member Alfalfa has been seeing a girl without their knowledge. They decide to put him on trial for his efforts! The gang has monetary problems, too. They need to build a new clubhouse, but have a hard time raising the money.

When a Man Loves a Woman *(pg. 26)*
(1994) Touchstone
Meg Ryan, Andy Garcia
Director: Luis Mandoki

Professionals call alcoholism a 'family disease' – and here's a film that shows why. Alice Green (Ryan) is an alcoholic with a husband (Garcia) and two young daughters. Showing clearly how alcoholism affects the fabric of marriage, *When a Man Loves a Woman* confronts issues and experiences that the 'recovered' alcoholic's family have to confront once the drinking ends.

Modern Times *(pg. 32)*
(1936) Chaplin/United Artists
Director: Charlie Chaplin

Made when everyone else was making 'talkies', *Modern Times* is Charlie Chaplin's last silent film (although it does have sound effects). In this satire of the mechanized world, and playing his best-known and possibly best-loved character – the Tramp – Chaplin plays a factory worker driven crazy by his dull and repetitive work. *Modern Times* is Chaplin at his best, drawing attention to the social issues of the day – with rip-roaring slapstick.

Babe: Pig in the City *(pg. 38)*
(1998) Universal
Director: George Miller

Using special effects to turn real animals into actors, director George Miller takes us – and sheep-pig Babe – into the dark and nightmarish city. Following a nasty accident to his 'boss', Farmer Hoggett, Babe and Mrs Hoggett must journey to the city to save the farm. Only one hotel will take animals, and it is here that Babe encounters four-legged friends (and enemies), and his quest begins.

Fairytale: A True Story *(pg. 44)*
(1997) Icon Productions
Director: Charles Sturridge

Loosely based on real events from early 20th-century England, this is the story of two young girls who apparently have the ability to photograph fairies in their garden. This catches the attention of the media and general public, and famous people like the great Sir Arthur Conan Doyle and Harry Houdini come to visit.

Star Trek III: The Search for Spock *(pg. 50)*
(1984) Paramount
William Shatner, Leonard Nimoy
Director: Leonard Nimoy

One of the many successful movies based upon the cult science fiction television series, *Star Trek III* continues the tradition of taking us boldly into the deepest recesses of the galaxy. This time Captain James T. Kirk (Shatner) must visit an unstable planet and try to recover his dead friend and colleague Spock's (Nimoy) body and 'essence', and bring him back to life.

Big Business *(pg. 56)*
(1929) MGM
Director: James W. Horne & Leo McCarey

This movie stars possibly the greatest comedy team of all time - Stan Laurel and Oliver Hardy. Dimwitted Stan and pompous Ollie are selling Christmas trees door to door, but business is slow. A simple disagreement with one customer turns into full-blown anarchy, and soon the comic duo's car has been destroyed, and the customer's house and garden have been reduced to a wasteland!

Trainspotting *(pg. 62)*
(1995) Figment/Noel Gay/Channel 4
Ewan McGregor, Robert Carlyle
Director: Danny Boyle

Set against the seedy bars and housing estates of Edinburgh, *Trainspotting* is an intense and often depressing look at disaffected youth and the nightmare of drug addiction. Mark Renton (McGregor) is trying to kick the heroin habit, but surrounded by friends and fellow addicts, he finds it hard. Finally he cleans up and moves to London, where he finds a job. But escaping from his previous life proves difficult.

Malcolm X *(pg. 68)*
(1992) Warner Brothers
Denzel Washington, Angela Bassett
Director: Spike Lee

Malcolm X (Washington) was the fiery African American leader, a cornerstone of the civil-rights movement, who believed in earning equality by any means necessary. His early life as a gangster-hustler put him in jail. Following this, Malcolm converted to Islam, took a pilgrimage to Mecca, and began his political mission. Spike Lee has created a masterpiece of storytelling, which shows the audience how a man found the power to change his life, and the lives of millions of others.

K-9 *(pg. 74)*
(1989) Universal
James Belushi
Director: Rod Daniel

In this comedy/action story, cop Michael Dooley (Belushi) is pursuing a drug-dealing criminal with little success. Enter Jerry Lee, a German Shepherd dog that has been trained to find drugs. Unfortunately, Jerry Lee has a mind of his own, and often has a less than helpful impact on Dooley's case.

Patriot Games *(pg. 80)*
(1992) Paramount
Harrison Ford, Anne Archer
Director: Phillip Noyce

Jack Ryan, hero of Tom Clancy's spy novels, foils a terrorist assassination attempt on a member of the British Royal family. As a result, Ryan and his family become targets for revenge. An intense, fast-moving film, *Patriot Games* is particularly good at highlighting the use of technology – especially spy satellites – in the world of modern espionage and counter-terrorism.

Bus Stop *(pg. 86)*
(1956) 20th Century Fox
Marilyn Monroe, Don Murray
Director: Joshua Logan

Starring the legendary Marilyn Monroe, *Bus Stop* is a suitable showcase for her many talents. When innocent rodeo cowboy Bo (Murray) falls in love with cafe singer Cherie (Monroe), she decides to run away to Los Angeles. Her lovesick suitor tracks her down and forces her to take a bus back to his hometown. It's winter and the road ahead is blocked, so they are forced to wait at a roadside café – Grace's Diner. A silverscreen classic that is funny and emotional in equal parts.

Elizabeth Taylor in London *(pg. 92)*
(1963)

Elizabeth Taylor grew from a doll-faced child starlet to become one of the silver screen's most striking beauties, not to mention a compelling actress and one of the world's most famous movie stars. She has been a natural magnet for publicity throughout her life and is one of the most photographed women in history. She even holds the record for the most appearances on the cover of *Life Magazine* (11). But lest her fame and notoriety overshadow her accomplishments, it is worth remembering that Taylor has received five Best Actresses nominations and two Oscar statuettes over the course of her amazing six-decade career. (source: www.reelclassics.com)

Patterns & Collocations

Accept

I accept that we shouldn't eat endangered species. 75
We should accept that there's no difference between 75
Most people accept that it's all right to eat plants. 75
Accept the last invitation. 11
... if she accepts your proposal. 53
Consider whether to accept or not. 53

Active

I was always active. 21
I prefer using my free time actively. 14

Adapt

I don't easily adapt to new ways of doing things. 20

Addict

What things are you addicted to? 64
I'd become addicted to alcohol. 62
Coffee is addictive. 64
Gambling can be addictive. 65

Admit

I admit that (you are right to some extent), but 76
I must admit he's a great guy! 8

Afraid

I'm afraid that's a typing mistake. 17
I want to be with people that aren't afraid to be different. . .87

Age

At what age should young people ...? 88
When I was your age, I thought nothing of 89
I like people that forget my age. 10
She doesn't look her age. 90
I wish she would act her age! She's so childish! 90
Fourteen can be a very difficult age. 90
It made me interested in things children of my age
    didn't normally 21
What do you think is the best age to get married? 68
The electronic age has taken the romance out of life. 81

All

We will all be able to work from home in the future. 84
Maybe we should all pay more tax. 27
I wonder what we will all be doing ten years from now. . . .50
It's wonderful to lie on the beach all day. 15
We fight all the time. 12
All they get is a hangover the next day. 62
My relatives are scattered all over the place. 26
After all, they made many sacrifices for us. 27
I've heard all kinds of people may try and get access. 80
He doesn't seem to mind at all. .8

Somebody's made it all up. 45
I love you with all my heart. 72
They all lived happily ever after. 23

Allow

We should be allowed to do a few things that are
    dangerous. 63

Almost

See if there are any books almost all the class have read. . . .23
My parents criticized me almost all the time. 26
I go out for dinner almost every night. 15
Almost everything will be done by robots. 51
I can go almost anywhere by bus or train. 42
They would give me almost anything I wanted. 26
I almost succeeded. 62

Always

I always drive slowly. 59
He's always so serious. 8
We should always move forward. 24
When I was a child I always used to study. 20
There's always the danger of being laid off. 32
I can always depend on him. 8
I bet it'll rain. It always does! 94

Animal

Many wild animals are now endangered. 74
It's wrong to eat any animal that's in danger of becoming
    extinct. 75
Lions and tigers are carnivorous animals. 78
Most domestic animals are very tame. 78
You're behaving like an animal! 78

Anybody

I couldn't go out with anybody that wasn't sensitive. 9
I hardly talk to anybody. 11
Hardly anybody buys me birthday presents. 52
Do you think expensive weddings make anybody happier? .70

Anything

They would give me almost anything I wanted. 26
It's very unlikely that anything like that will happen. 50
Are you doing anything on Monday night? 11
You don't know anything about computers. 83

Anywhere

I can go almost anywhere by bus or train. 42
If I go anywhere, I like to take a long trip. 92
It doesn't get us anywhere. 87

Appreciate

We don't appreciate them. 69

Patterns & Collocations

Patterns & Collocations

Do

When we have nothing to do, we can throw stones
   at the buses. 29
I'd be prepared to do a lot of overtime. 33
I'll do my best. 36
Many people don't do enough exercise. 57
It didn't do too much damage. 80
I need this translation done by tomorrow night. 36
I wonder what we will all be doing ten years from now? ...50

Doubt

I doubt it. 68
I doubt if many people get long enough vacations
   to do that. 93

Down

There's a zebra crossing further down the street. 42
I'm trying to cut down on laundry bills. 24
Cars sometimes break down. 56
All the computers at school are down for some reason. 84
Deep down, you probably want the same things as me. 9
They really help me calm down. 14
It comes down to the level of intelligence of what we eat. ..75
The older generation talks down to me. 86
Why don't you find a good job and settle down? 87

Dream

I dream of living in a large house with a garden. 53
Going to Hawaii was just like a wonderful dream. 54
I always dreamed of having my own business and the
   dream came true. 54
I achieved my dream of spending a year in Australia. 54
Analyze her dream. 47

Duty

It's our duty to look after our parents when they get older. .27

Earn

I'll probably be trying to earn enough money to
   support my family. 50

Easily

I easily get bored. 9
I don't easily adapt to new ways of doing things. 20
When expensive things come too easily, we don't
   appreciate them. 69

Easy

It's easy to do. 80
Take it easy. 18
It'd be easier to use a saucepan. 66
It's easy (for me) to understand why she did it. 64
Finding a partner is not as easy as it seems. 70
It's easy when you know how. 60

Effective / effectively

People like that are more effective in changing society. 87
We'll be able to prevent it more effectively. 51

Else

Everybody else was having a party. 48
Nobody else used that room. 21
I get bored with people that want to be like everybody else. 87

E-mail

Computers are useful for sending e-mails. 83
I haven't been able to access my e-mail for a few days. 84
I receive at least twenty e-mails every day. 84
May I use this computer to check my e-mail? 84

End

They end up as alcoholics. 62

Enough

If I ..., there wouldn't be enough time to build a
   happy home. 33
I'll probably be trying to earn enough money to
   support my family. 50
We can find a way if we try hard enough. 27
There just aren't enough exciting opportuntites. 39
Is there enough space in the living room for my tank of
   piranha? 29
There isn't enough room to swing a cat. 78
Many people don't do enough exercise. 57
I don't have enough confidence to go off into the
   countryside ... .93

Even

I'm very bad at teamwork, even when I play soccer. 45
I'm not even an adolescent any more. 86
They spend even more on their honeymoons. 69
It's normal to live in different cities or even in different
   countries. 27
Everybody makes mistakes. Even bosses do! 35
Even though it has such a large population, I feel so lonely. 38
We might even be governed by robots. 51
Even these days this can be a very good system. 68
He never even considers having an affair. 72

Everybody

Everybody else was having a party. 48
Everybody will be much happier than now. 51
If everybody traveled more, there wouldn't be any wars. ..96
Everybody makes mistakes. 35
We've arranged a trip to Hawaii. Everybody's going! 18

Expect / expectations

I expect I'll be doing a normal nine-to-five job. 50
Old people who expect to live with ... are being selfish. ..27
Parents may expect too much. 26
... one or the other of the couple has unrealistic
   expectations. 68

Patterns & Collocations

Patterns & Collocations

Patterns & Collocations

There's a local restaurant that's very good. 18
It's a very traditional restaurant so we usually dress up. 18

Rid
It's a good way to get rid of stress. 57

Right
If you agree that I'm right, I'll agree that you're wrong. 90
Perhaps they were right. .81
Two wrongs don't make a right. 90
It's all right to eat plants. 75
We have a right to live our own lives. 86
To what extent should smokers respect the rights of
   non smokers? 64

Routine
Cities offer a chance to escape from a routine life. 39

Run
We've just run out of champagne. 17
We've run out of time. 18
Dancers run in the family. 30

Same
They're learning a lot at the same time. 81
The same way as short cows. .77
Humans and other animals are basically the same. 78
I get bored when I'm with people that do the same thing
   every day. 87
You probably want the same things as me. 9
Too many of them follow the same fashions. 90
We always go to the same place for our family vacation. . . .96
We're definitely on the same wavelength. 48
Same sex marriages should be just as acceptable. 72

Say
It should say 'duck'. 17
The only good thing I can say about the city is that it's
   good for 38
It's amazing that so much of what she said has come true. .44
Whatever she said would stand a good chance of
   coming true. 44
You say that now, but after we get married you'll forget
   what you said. 53
That's just what I was going to say. 48
Managers don't listen to what we have to say. 87
He never listens to a word we say. 90
It's often said that travel broadens the mind. 93

Scattered
It may be true that many families can't help becoming
   scattered. 27
My relatives are scattered all over the place. 26

See
I went to see a fortune teller. 44

I didn't see the sign. 66
I love seeing the famous sights of London, Rio de Janeiro ... 93
You might not see a lot of each other. 33
What is there to see in London? 41
Whenever I see a dachshund I smile. 77
I see what you mean. 16

Seem
Our ideas may sometimes seem too radical. 86
It seems like (as if) none of you spent much time with
   adults. 21
It seems to be pretty accurate. 45
He doesn't seem to mind at all. 8
It may not seem like it, but 15
Nothing seems to work. 65
It's not as crazy as it seems. .69

-Self
He just prefers being by himself. 8
I just want to be free to be myself. 26
I want to leave home and live by myself. 30
Make yourself at home. 30
Pull yourself together! 47

Sense
He doesn't have much of a sense of humor. 8
It doesn't make sense to ban drugs like marijuana. 63

Serious
I might change my mind if I have a serious relationship. . . .9
Maybe that's why I'm quite a serious person. 21
You don't seriously think the Dodgers will win? 54

Share
I'd like to share an apartment with Tomoko. 94

Situation
Talk about the general situation in your family. 28

Sorry
I'm sorry, I'm busy on Monday. 11
I'm extremely sorry, sir/madam. 17
I'm sorry to tell you at/on such short notice. 36
I just feel sorry for people who go to big cities. 39

Sound
It sounds like (as if) you don't have much fun! 20

Space
Is there enough space in the living room? 29

Spend
I've spent six years at university taking medicine. 88
I spent most of my time indoors. 21
I spend too much money on fashionable clothes. 28
They spend all their time discussing pop music. 39

Patterns & Collocations

Stand
I can't stand my brother-in-law. 26
Whatever she said would stand a good chance of
   coming true. 44
Type B people stand back from the world around them. . . .45

Start
I've made a lot of new friends since I started learning
   English. 12
You'll probably start looking for a lot of sensitive friends. . . .9

Still
You can still stay with a group of people. 93

Story
I'll tell you a story. 24
This is a true story. 24
I used to love reading fairy stories. 24

Stress
It's a good way to get rid of stress. 57
Driving's one of the biggest causes of stress. 57
I know that can be stressful. 57
I can understand people ... when they are having a lot of
   stress. 62

Suit
That kind of job wouldn't suit me. 33
Blue doesn't suit me. 34
Maybe we're not suitable. 71

Supposed
People who have O type are supposed to be individualistic. 45
What am I supposed to be like? .45

Sure
I'm not sure. 28
I'm sure I'd hate working for a large corporation. 32
Are you sure you prefer to live in the country? 40
Make sure it doesn't happen again! 41
I'm not sure what love really is. .46
I'm not sure whether intelligence should be the
   deciding factor. 75

Take
I like to take care of my pets. 14
Take it easy. 18
I think I take after my father. 30
It only takes twenty minutes to get to work. 38
It sometimes takes hours to commute to work. 38
I prefer to take short trips 92
I don't know why so many people are taken in by this
   kind of nonsense. 45
They shouldn't take all the fun out of our lives. 63
Take these tablets three times a day. 65
Computers will take over the world. 84

I don't take out any insurance. 92
I took time off work to go to the hospital. 36

Talk
We talk about what our friends are doing. 17
I hardly talk to anybody. 11
I'm talking about drives in the countryside. 57
You don't know what you are talking about! 58

Technology
He'll be good at handling all the new technology. 81
My new computer uses all the latest technology. 84
I'd like to take a course in Information Technology. 84
There's a lot of very advanced technology in the
   production process. 84

Tell
I wish he would tell a few jokes. .8
I'll tell you a story. 24
Tell me more about why you like helicopters so much. . . .35
I told you to take that gorilla to the zoo. 40
We can tell a lot about a person's character from their
   blood type. 45
Could you tell me a little about the castle's history? 95

Temptation
I couldn't resist the temptation to play a computer game. . .66
I try hard to keep away from temptation. 66
I gave in to temptation and had a large piece of
   chocolate cake. 66

Tend
I tend to rush around doing a lot of things. 14
Older people tend to be conservative. 88
Do you tend to look at people younger than you as
   immature? 88

Thing
There are so many other things to do. 15
I don't easily adapt to new ways of doing things. 20
The only thing he ever thought about was soccer. 21
The only good thing I can say about the city is that it's
   good for 38
The surprising thing about living in the city is 38
They may seem to do the same thing every day. 87
They are gradually gaining the experience and power to
   improve things. 87
You must be too exhausted to do that kind of thing. 15
What kinds of things do you talk about? 26
I don't need those kinds of things. 87

Think
I think you'll regret it later. 20
Do you think some people can predict the future? 46
Don't you think we need a chance to experience city life? . .39
They think they are so clever. 62

Patterns & Collocations

About the Author

David Paul was born in Weymouth, UK, went to secondary school in Dorchester, and graduated with an MA in Social and Political Science from Trinity Hall, Cambridge University.

After teaching EFL in the UK, he went to teach in Hiroshima in 1980 and has been based there ever since. In 1982, he began his own language school, 'David English House', which became the largest school in the area after a few years.

Since 1981, he has written a number of best-selling course books, run teacher training courses throughout East Asia, set up franchise teacher training centers in Korea and Thailand, and been a plenary or featured speaker at many major conferences in the region.